Climb aboard and buckle up. It's going to be a bumpy ride.

The Adventures of Priscilla, Queen of the Desert is the funniest movie to emerge from the outback of Australia in years, and Al Clark was involved in the creation of it—from conception to triumphant success. He and director Stephan Elliott survived various natural disasters and acts of God, such as floods, earthquakes, bushfires, bomb threats, film festivals, confused critics, the outré L.A. bar scene, and power lunches, lurching from crisis to crisis to make the most hysterical film of the year.

With wry humor and a true dedication to the art of modern moviemaking, Al Clark tells the story behind the marabou feathers and multicolored sequins of the film that has sparked a whirlwind of excitement across the world and been hailed as a masterpiece of its genre.

AL CLARK, writer and film producer, began his career as a journalist in London. His British production credits include *Aria, Absolute Beginners,* and *Gothic.* In Australia, he was executive producer of George Ogilvie's *The Crossing,* and produced Stephan Elliott's *The Adventures of Priscilla, Queen of the Desert.* He currently makes his home in Sydney, Australia.

Making Priscilla

Al Clark

A PLUME BOOK

Preceding page: Terence Stamp as Bernadette, photographed by Elise Lockwood

PLUME
Published by the Penguin Group
Penguin Books USA Inc., 375 Hudson Street,
New York, New York 10014, U.S.A.
Penguin Books Ltd, 27 Wrights Lane,
London W8 5TZ, England
Penguin Books Australia Ltd, Ringwood,
Victoria, Australia
Penguin Books Canada Ltd, 10 Alcorn Avenue,
Toronto, Ontario, Canada M4V 3B2
Penguin Books (N.Z.) Ltd, 182–190 Wairau Road,
Auckland 10, New Zealand

Penguin Books Ltd, Registered Offices:
Harmondsworth, Middlesex, England

Published by Plume, an imprint of Dutton Signet,
a division of Penguin Books USA Inc.
First published in 1994 by Penguin Books Australia.

First Plume Printing, February, 1995
10 9 8 7 6 5 4 3 2 1

 REGISTERED TRADEMARK—MARCA REGISTRADA

ISBN 0-452-27484-2

Printed in the United States of America

For Andrena and Rachel

Acknowledgements

Thanks to all the cast and crew for their contributions to the adventure, particularly to the core group – Brian Breheny, Tim Chappel, Lizzy Gardiner, Colin Gibson and Grant Lee – whose allegiance began long before we could pay them; to Elise Lockwood, Richard Blanshard and my colleague Michael Hamlyn for their photographs; to Adam Plate at the Pink Roadhouse on the Oodnadatta Track for his map; to Rebel Penfold-Russell and Latent Image, under whose roof much of this was written; to Bob Sessions and Kathy Hope at Penguin, for suggesting and navigating it respectively, and to Phillip Adams, who encouraged me to write again; finally, to Stephan Elliott, the sheer scale of whose folly made all of ours flourish.

A.C.

Contents

The Beginning

It is one-thirty in the morning when the call comes through.

In the part of the imagination where dread lives, these calls only occur in the middle of the night, and on more occasions over the years than I wish I could remember I have stumbled, numb and dazed, in the dark towards the telephone to find that it is just somebody from another country who has no idea what time it is in Sydney. Nobody ever knows what time it is in Sydney, except for those who live there, and they know far too well.

The caller, from London, has been given my number by the only person in Sydney or anywhere else who knows where I am staying that night. He has woken the manager of a motel on the high street of Cottonwood, Arizona, a sepulchrally quiet western town full of tumbleweed and old ghosts, and the manager has walked down to his office and switched through the call.

It begins with the four words every child with a developed sense of loss grows up to fear the most: your father is dead.

The daughter of the British actor Patrick Magee, who died in 1982, once told me that soon after his demise she met the daughter of Patrick MacNee, who was in *The Avengers*. On the day that Patrick Magee died, Patrick MacNee's daughter was staying at her father's house in

Palm Springs while he was away appearing in a stage play in Australia. A reporter from one of the American tabloids called to ask how she felt about her father's death. 'But he can't be dead,' she protested. 'He's in Australia. I spoke to him on the phone half an hour ago.' The reporter would not be overridden. 'Oh, he's dead,' he reassured her. 'It's the time difference.'

October 1992. I am in America for two reasons. One is that my wife Andrena Finlay, who has produced a film called *Frauds*, is in Los Angeles with its writer-director Stephan Elliott, engaged in what began as a co-operative venture but is deteriorating into a war of wills. After viewing the director's cut of the movie on tape, the US co-financiers Live Entertainment, a video distribution company allied to the high-rolling Carolco Pictures, have made it a condition of their acceptance (and consequent payment of the substantial sum due on delivery) that the picture is re-edited under their supervision and at their expense. The understanding is that this will be done in consultation with, and with the participation of the writer-director, but his increasing exasperation with what they are doing to the film – particularly the first two reels – is making him a combative collaborator, and it is being made clear in various ways that he is not welcome in the cutting room except when called in to review edited sequences.

The other – heightened by the disappointed incomprehension which Sydney people involuntarily display to somebody who has forgone his status as a glamorous outsider – is that I feel increasingly isolated living in Australia, where I moved because of marriage, because my birthday is a national holiday there, and because it is the only country in the world to have lost a prime minister surfing.

As a resourceful film producer and executive who also speaks fluent Spanish, it seems appropriate that I should consider moving to a Spanish-speaking city which is also the centre of the movie business. I have an encyclopaedic knowledge of film history, which may be a distinction in a place where the majority of executives think of *The Breakfast Club* as an old movie, and I do my own reading, which might make me unique.

Coverage – the synopsis and reader's assessment prepared when a novel or a screenplay arrives in the offices of a film production company – is virtually a trading currency in Hollywood. If one's 'material' receives positive coverage, word travels and so does the coverage, which becomes a kind of talisman. Negative coverage, on the other hand, can kill a good screenplay because it means that only the incorrigibly curious will bother to read it.

Most coverage is itself practically unreadable, saturated with the arcane vernacular of assessors, with their beats, turning points and throughlines. It is also, by its very nature, highly unreliable. (A studio head who had skimmed the coverage of a project finally read the script when the picture, ready to start shooting, came to him for final approval. 'The guy's a loser,' he complained about the main character before pulling the plug on the movie. 'It didn't say *that* in the coverage.') Perhaps the most devastatingly sparse coverage of all was provided by Gore Vidal to a producer who approached him with a screenplay which required, the producer claimed, 'a polish'. Vidal read it. 'You think the script needs a polish,' he replied.

'I think it needs a trip to Lourdes.'

In addition to visiting the people I know already, I arrange to see a few I have never met. Apart from a desire to defy the odds by dreaming up a genuinely original game show, I do not have much interest in television, which, to paraphrase Quentin Crisp, both diminishes and domesticates the scale of our fantasies. But I have never come across an American TV executive before, and I feel it is time that I did, just in case the game show materialises.

A man at NBC informs me that their mini-series and telemovies are 'concept driven'. Are there any concepts, I ask, that they have no interest in driving? 'Satanism, abortion, homosexuality. We don't do those. And,' he adds archly, 'the disease of the week is currently in remission.' So at whom were these shows aimed? 'Our demographic is 18 to 49,' he replies. A pause. 'Which you could say isn't really a demographic at all.'

While it is not the Latino link I could be looking for, I meet two interesting Mexicans within a few hours. An actor from Ensenada, catching his breath in the lobby of the cable network Showtime, following a five-hour drive to deliver in person an audition showreel for Jim McBride's *The Wrong Man* which he stayed up all night preparing with two video players linked up in his living room; and a video distributor who tells me about a friend in Mexico City, the theatrical distributor of the film *Alligator 2*, who calls an exhibitor to enquire about the first day's results at the box office. The exhibitor tells him that there has been no business. The distributor, conceding that the picture is not a blockbuster, asks how much money it took. 'I said no business,' replies the exhibitor, 'I mean not a single dollar, *not a ticket sold.*'

I enjoy the freewheeling, but around the time that I find myself discussing with a senior executive at Universal whether he should take a deli sandwich or a falafel to the baseball game that evening it occurs to me that perhaps what I should be pitching to people here – the home of the sporting metaphor in business – is something a little more specific than the ability to give an epigrammatic shape to a random thought.

The pitch is a crucial kick-start to the labyrinthine process of getting a picture made, and while there are no unconditional laws, the shorter it is the more likely it is to be effective. The story should take no longer than two minutes, the high concept summary – which invariably will include the title of a recent hit movie – about five seconds. As *Die Hard* epitomises the successful action-thriller franchise which everybody seeks to emulate, *Under Siege* would almost certainly have been pitched as *Die Hard* on a battleship, and *Speed* as *Die Hard* on a bus, although I cherish the idea of *Die Hard* at a wedding, or *Die Hard* at a bar mitzvah. The two best pitches I have heard of were both made at the same studio, Universal. The director Ivan Reitman is reported to have settled in the president's office, waited for silence, said 'Schwarzenegger. De Vito. *Twins*' and then got up to leave. The producer David Permut was even briefer. He entered escorting Dan Ackroyd, sat him in an armchair and stood behind it pointing at Ackroyd's head while humming the first four notes of the *Dragnet* theme.

At the 1991 Cannes Film Festival seventeen months earlier, while waiting for Phil Collins' vacillating commitment to star in *Frauds* to trigger the film's funding,

Stephan and Andrena went around pitching a musical comedy about two drag queens and a transsexual driving across Australia in a bus. It was called *The Adventures of Priscilla, Queen of the Desert*, which Stephan had written a couple of weeks before the festival, so that he would have something else to talk about while he was there.

His verbal pitch to a series of increasingly bewildered distributors was absolutely hilarious, but his attempts at 'director's notes', full of bad grammar and flaccid hyperbole, were comical for a different reason. Invoking Dusan Makavejev and Bill Bennett – the only two directors with whom he had worked as an assistant who were known to Cannes regulars – he described a drag queen as 'an extremely amusing and very much neglected member of today's society,' then added, with a perfunctory sting for the international marketplace, 'that they exist, enthral, amuse and entertain people of all races in all corners of the globe.'

After Cannes he wrote another 'director's note': 'Nobody could anticipate the reaction. The recording and newly formed film production giant PolyGram International snapped up the concept within hours. Before I could draw a breath, England's unstoppable "hit factory" Stock/Aitken/Waterman agreed to produce all the music for the film's production numbers and allow us access to their artists for cameos. A very major international star has expressed keen interest in playing the leading drag queen.'

In the long interlude since then, *Frauds* has been made and *Priscilla*, which threatened to become trapped in the congested corporate arteries of PolyGram, has been navigated through them, first by Sarah Radclyffe at the subsidiary Working Title; then, after her departure from the company, by Michael Hamlyn, a producer who had been working there and a friend of INXS singer Michael Hutchence, 'the very major international star' to whom Stephan alluded in his boast. Meanwhile, Andrena has brought in the Australian government-backed funding body the Film Finance Corporation (FFC), and a deal has been agreed in principle, subject to many conditions still to be negotiated, the cardinal one being casting.

Even in its still incomplete state, *Frauds* strikes me as the most confident first film I have seen, and one of the most original. If there is a presiding spirit, it is that of a more bad-tempered Tim Burton. It is not a traditional comedy (though it has many comic elements, black and otherwise) or an orthodox thriller (despite moments when it masquerades as one), and Phil Collins' affable image takes a darkly malevolent turn. Above all, it is a film full of bold strokes and colours, not a *beige* picture or one of those festival movies, ponderous yet entirely without gravity, that could easily have been directed by a social worker. Some have complained about its gleeful cruelty, about its lack of compassion towards its characters, but despite its flaws it is the most idiosyncratic first feature from an antipodean director since Jane Campion's *Sweetie*.

The script of *Priscilla* is more broadly comedic in tone, as well as being, in its latter stages, quite touching, a quality intensified by the total absence of ingratiation employed to achieve it. It is inhabited by people with a recognisable 'voice', developed individuals who do not exist solely to propel the needs of the narrative. As Jonathan Demme did in his 80s' comedies, particularly *Something Wild*, Stephan transcends the preoccupation with having characters merely be funny: he also creates a funny world for them to drift through, trying to find their bearings.

He gave me a copy to read at the time he first wrote it, and apart from a middle act – subsequently revised – that lost its pulse beat and momentum, lapsing too often into dreary caricature, it felt remarkably complete, with a consistently high standard of abuse exchanged by the bickering protagonists.

If the directors I have worked with have had anything in common other than their distinctiveness, it is that they aspired to be – in some cases already were – real movie makers, in love with the medium, intoxicated with exploiting it and incapable of confusing it with any other. When I produced films in the UK in the mid 80s, its cinema was largely suffocated by literary emphasis, subdued emotions, visual restraint. It was rarely surreal, playful or sexually charged. At its worst, watching it was rather like downing a magnum of chloroform. While many Australian pictures of the period were equally soporific and middlebrow, one felt at least an impatient energy at work behind the decorum, even if the cringing fear of making a mess on the carpet was still predominant.

It is evident that Stephan does want to make a mess on the carpet, and preferably to spread it around the house as well. He certainly has talent, although I am not yet sure that it is matched by judgement. Perhaps that is what I am supposed to contribute. When he and Andrena propose that I replace her as the producer of *Priscilla*, I am excited by the challenge.

Other than dreary expediency, there are many complex and overlapping reasons for wanting to make a particular film. Because it takes so long, is sometimes so poorly paid and is frequently the incubator of so much conflict, it requires a tonic which gives buoyancy to the banality of the process, a sense of mission which keeps one in a state of resolute enchantment through the sheer drudgery required to make the movie happen.

For me, the key is always a haunting image, the one around which the picture will revolve. In the case of *Priscilla*, it is a series of images, which will eventually become the film's central montage: one drag queen rehearses a musical number in solitude against a vast desert backdrop, while another applies a coat of lavender paint over graffiti on the bus, and the third walks across the Outback to find help.

Stephan has never been to a drag show outside of Australia, so I take him to one. There is a club in Los Angeles called The Plaza, which I first visited because someone told me it was full of Mexican men in gingham dresses lip-synching to songs from *Oklahoma*. It turns out to be family night, which means it is simultaneously more sedate and more surreal, with several generations in attendance witnessing the subversion of south-of-the-border standards by guys with five o'clock shadows dressed up like Carmen Miranda. One drag queen has decided to play to the Anglo gallery. Precision miming to Dionne Warwick's heroically drippy 'I Know I'll Never Love This Way Again', she uses the pause before the triumphant final chorus to whisper 'thank you,' then launches into the exhilarating coda. It really brings the *hacienda* down.

After my father's funeral in Scotland – on a cold windswept hill under bruised Ayrshire skies – I fly back to Australia to begin building the *Priscilla* jigsaw.

We have a provisional AUS$2.7 million, and six weeks in which to make a road movie with several elaborate musical production numbers. It is the budget and schedule of a chamber drama set in the smallest chamber of the house, but it is all we have and we are going to make the most of it. Stephan and I are working for a rock-bottom $50,000 each, as is Michael Hamlyn, who will represent PolyGram's interests on the production. Rebel Penfold-Russell receives five thousand dollars less as executive producer, and her company Latent Image – which has, with a small contribution from the New South Wales Film and Television Office (NSWFTO), supported the development of the picture to date – is allocated a small overhead as well as recovering its out-of-pocket costs.

There is so little money to pay the crew that the only way we can afford to employ the people we want is to offer key personnel participation in the film's profits as compensation for their low salaries. Although we do not plan to start principal photography until the end of April 1993 – after the Outback temperatures have become more tolerable, but before the approach of winter diminishes the length of the shooting day – we have a great deal to do in the intervening six months, and it is important to build a solid team that will make itself available at the time.

Only a few crew positions are filled in advance. The director of photography will be Brian Breheny, who shot Stephan's calling-card shorts *Fast* and *The Agreement*, and was to do *Frauds* until the FFC would not accept a new cinematographer working with a first-time feature director; and Grant Lee, a long-time friend of Stephan's who worked in the art department of *Frauds*, will learn about producing films by working as my assistant, without pay until the start of pre-production. Provided they are people we can afford, Brian will also choose the gaffer and grip: apart from his small camera crew, they are the people who will most affect his contribution to the film.

To design the costumes, Stephan wants Lizzy Gardiner and Tim Chappel, who are working on the television show *E Street*, because they know how to make a modest wardrobe budget – for a film such as this, an absurdly minimal one – go a long way, and because they understand contemporary drag. There is a realm of transvestism which is still entrenched in the world of ball gowns, Barbra Streisand and Shirley Bassey, with whom one of the characters in this draft of the script is besotted. But increasingly drag has become much more a confrontational performance art, with costumes that correspondingly take it into another dimension.

Stephan was once infatuated with Lizzy, who spurned him for another man, so our meeting begins with a cathartic tirade on the subject, rising to an intensity which leaves her, Tim and me open-mouthed in astonished silence. When it is over, we talk about costumes. Tim has just designed the clothes for a trio of lissom poppets called The Teen Queens, whose launch as a singing act was an appearance on *E Street*. On the same day that I see them perform under the noon sun in the courtyard of the Bondi Pavilion, they turn up six hours later lip-synching (same act, change of outfits) in the amphitheatre at Darling Harbour outside a wedding reception I am attending. Inside, after the cutting of the cake, I invite a man I have never met before who is sitting at the same table to join me on stage for a karaoke duet of 'I Say a Little Prayer'. I am unable to remember which one of us sings the deathless couplet 'Back-combing my hair now/and wondering what dress to wear now', but the ease of my performance is prompting some concern that I may be approaching my new duties a little too enthusiastically.

We interview production managers, assistant directors, editors, production designers, and we laugh constantly. The whole thing is an amusement, we have decided, to be approached with a complete disregard for hindrance. If anybody looks perturbed when we mention money, we go on to the next person. We tell everybody that we will be making the movie like a guerilla operation working its way across country – shoot and move on. One prospective production designer, misunderstanding it to be a gorilla movie, tells us we are going to find it difficult making a picture about three apes in dresses driving across the desert.

Although we have many frivolous casting ideas – which mostly involve getting particular media celebrities, chat show hosts and folk heroes to make sequined fools of themselves – we have one serious one. The only bankable young actor in Australia at this moment is Paul Mercurio, the star of *Strictly Ballroom*, and although Mercurio has recently started a dance company to which he is giving most of his attention, we know that he will soon be looking for another film role. Stephan and he have lunch during a break in dance rehearsals, and Stephan returns with the impression that – despite Mercurio's obvious anxiety about playing a drag queen in his second film after playing a dancer in his first – he is sufficiently fascinated to give us a realistic chance of securing him. If Michael Hutchence is to play Tick, the thirtysomething borderline straight with the wife and child, Mercurio could play the young bitchy scene-queen Adam. To have Australia's pre-eminent pop star and actor appearing together on screen would certainly be an achievement for a movie whose production company is surrendering most of its eventual profits to get it made at all.

At this stage, the only location that we must have is Ayers Rock – Australia's counterpart of, say, Stonehenge or Monument Valley – which is climbed by the protagonists in full drag at the climax of the movie. It is the Northern Territory office of the Australian National Parks and Wildlife Service (ANPWS) that issues the guidelines and, when inclined, grants the permissions, but it is the Aboriginal Mutitjulu Community – always referred to with deferential solemnity as 'the traditional owners' – which makes the decisions, and it is someone called the Community Park Liaison Officer who acts as a go-between.

I write to him and enclose a copy of the script. Even a delirious optimist would find it difficult to view our chances as remotely promising. A glance through the guidelines reveals that shooting from the air, within a certain radius and altitude, is not permitted, so there can be no triumphant helicopter shot at the end of the climb. And I note that Aboriginal traditions applied to the rock distinguish between sites which men alone are permitted to see, and those restricted to women only. In the context of this, three drag queens would certainly prompt a confused reaction.

With a location survey planned for the week before Christmas, my letter begins by pre-empting what I think their first reaction will be: 'We are well aware that you probably don't get many requests to film men in dresses climbing the rock.' Then I ramble a little about how, in addition to being funny and benevolent, our script has an important message about acceptance between people generally, and between minorities in particular. This is the truth, but the leaden sanctimony of it make me feel slightly nauseated.

Two weeks later our request is rejected. Many people appear to have discussed it – the chairman and other members of the Mutitjulu Community, the chairman of the Uluru Board of Management, the Uluru National Park Manager, the director of ANPWS Northern Operations – and their consensus view is that we do not fit the bill, outlining criteria which only a documentary could fulfil. The only movie in the past decade to have received permission to film around the rock was *Evil Angels* (known outside Australia as *A Cry in the Dark*) and that was rumoured to have required intervention from circles as high as the Prime Minister's office. We will ask again.

For a film of our budget to obtain the Australian certification necessary to release FFC funds, we are allowed only one foreign actor in the event that our Australian stars do not materialise. On the flight to Los Angeles, where Stephan is supervising the sound preparation for *Frauds*, I have what I consider a brilliant casting idea: David Bowie. I knew Bowie in the mid 80s – when we discussed the possibility of him writing the score for *Nineteen Eighty-Four*, and he appeared briefly but winningly in another film with which I was involved, *Absolute Beginners* – but I did not see him again until late 1989, when he played me some songs he was recording in Sydney at the time, and gave me one to use over the end titles of *The Crossing*, the picture I was then working on. He is a wonderful man but difficult to track down. His manager tells me he is finishing his first solo album for over five years and that it would be better not to distract him for a while.

Although I am on the way to London to see Michael Hamlyn, PolyGram's film-sales arm Manifesto and PWL Records about *Priscilla*, my airline ticket and expenses are being paid for by a television company. The deal is that I have to make small talk on a sofa with Michael Parkinson, which I have always wanted to do anyway, during several minutes of prime-time TV on the pilot of a show called *Surprise Party* – a rowdier variation on *This Is Your Life*, with champagne and paper hats – the subject of whose first surprise party was my employer for thirteen years, Richard Branson. I am not sure that I want to spend the rest of my life appearing in the computer files of television researchers as an 'expert' on Richard Branson's early years in the record business, but I suppose there are worse places to be.

My hotel is just around the corner from Branson's house, so during the day before the recording I do everything short of adopting a beard and dark glasses to avoid identification, only to find myself seated at the same table as him at a wedding reception. It is difficult to say which of us is more surprised to see the other, and I am relieved that there is no karaoke machine to distract us. I tell him I am in London to finalise some business in connection with a movie I am producing about drag queens driving across the Australian desert in a bus, and he nods at me distractedly as if the long time we spent together was just an apprenticeship for me losing my marbles.

After the recording itself, when Branson ritually pours

champagne all over me as if he has not already ruined enough of my clothes in the past, I am chatting to John Hurt, whom I have not seen since the Cannes premiere of *Aria* in 1987. It occurs to me that he might be an appropriate Bernadette, the older transsexual, but seconds before I am about to mention it I remember that he has just finished playing a role in drag in Gus Van Sant's *Even Cowgirls Get The Blues*, so we confine ourselves to the kind of drunken reminiscing which is more appropriate to the event.

While some of the matters that I need to resolve with Hamlyn and PolyGram are routine – which of their companies is to be the contracting party and funding entity, can the money be cash-flowed in Australian dollars, and so on – others require more discussion. We are absolutely resolute that whichever party sells the Australian distribution rights should not take a commission, and there is the question of what is a fair premium on PolyGram's investment, if taking a premium on a low-budget film on which one also has sales rights can be said to be fair at all. The FFC, who would prefer not to charge a premium at all, will take whatever PolyGram do. Sales commissions, expenses, distribution fees, premiums: these, and the accounting procedures which reinforce them, are the hidden enemies of a film ever going into profit, which is why stars and directors who are in a position to jump the queue insist on gross points from first dollar, thereby eroding net profits – which Eddie Murphy once called 'monkey points' – even further.

I visit David Howells at PWL and we try to move the soundtrack deal along. The principles are that PWL will pay all the synchronisation fees due to the artist, recording company and publisher of any song used in the film; that they will pay the costs of remixes and rerecordings for the movie and corresponding soundtrack album; that they will pay us a royalty after recoupment of costs; and that we will pay them a percentage of the film's profits. It is almost revolutionary in its simplicity, and only the high costs being quoted are debated. I ask if it is possible for the soundtrack album to be released through PolyGram: it is not, as PWL has a worldwide distribution deal with Warner. This increases pressure on me to secure good terms. Our principal investors have a music division which is not getting the soundtrack rights, so if I am unable to conclude an outside deal that is attractive to them as film financiers, it makes it more difficult to convince them that their record company should not have it.

I fly back to Los Angeles, where the final sound mix of *Frauds* is nearly completed. I am perturbed by how little progress we have made with casting, and I am keen to move past the dithering of Hutchence and Mercurio to somebody who is going to commit. I bump into Alan Parker – whom I once tried to get to direct a musical version of *Wuthering Heights* called *Total Eclipse of the Heart* – doing some Christmas shopping at the Beverly Centre. I remark how difficult it is going to be to find a male actor with enough nerve to play a woman. 'Never mind nerve,' he scoffs, 'the difficulty will be finding an actor with enough *acting ability* to play a woman.'

There is a screening of *Frauds* in a San Fernando Valley mixing theatre large enough to accommodate a football game, attended by Phil Collins and associates, the sales agents J&M and the two investors from Live Entertainment. One of them dislikes the film so much by now that he slips out a third of the way into the picture and comes back in time for the end. The other one comments that the strange aquatic sound effects, which Stephan has added because of their unsettling quality, just made her want to go to the toilet. Everybody has had enough.

Everybody, that is, but Stephan, who stays on for a few days to supervise the final details. He is dauntingly hyperactive, and when I meet him for a drink to hand over his Christmas present – a biography of the cross-dressing director Edward Wood – before catching the plane to Sydney, I wish that he were coming with me so that he could break the cycle. The next time I see him he will look quite different.

It is the evening of Christmas Day. Stephan's flight has arrived that morning, but uncharacteristically he has not called. We are at the annual 'orphans' Christmas', which is usually held in whatever house he is living each Christmas for friends who have no parents, or whose parents live somewhere else, or who simply do not like their parents much. As many of these friends have at some time worked in the catering business, the food is always delicious and prepared without fuss, the standard of banter reliably high.

Tonight, however, the host is missing. He is upstairs in bed, and he is not in good shape. The year of continuous pressure he has been under, exacerbated by all the conflicts of defending *Frauds* against potential damage, has resulted in his arrival at the chequered flag in a state of some dislocation. His tension is such that at times he is unable to breathe, bringing on an anxiety attack which in turn makes it even more difficult for him to breathe. He is worried about going into pre-production on *Priscilla* in this kind of state. It is a concern that I share. I tell him he should take a holiday and not worry about the movie. If he does not do so, there will be no picture anyway. So he goes skiing in Europe with Grant. I revise the schedule, allowing for his absence until mid-February.

I am told that the NSWFTO, in addition to their script development function, have recently announced funds to invest in production, so we apply for some to supplement our pitiful budget. We have learned that the post-production house Apocalypse are unable to provide certain sound services as part of their facilities investment – which means we need more cash to pay for them – and the amount we have allocated to the cast is quite risible.

The NSWFTO's initial response is a curious, disturbingly American one: they send me coverage. Although their assessment is not as crucifying as one made by the Australian Film Commission when it was rejected by them after Cannes 1991 (citing stereotyped characters, political incorrectness and the view that Stephan's short films were 'deeply shallow'), it is quite scornful. Remembering my own maxim about coverage being a kind of trading currency, I find the reader's report sent to us by the ICM agency in Los Angeles and decide that the only pertinent reply is to make a comparison between them, if for no other reason than to illustrate how difficult it is to deal with these completely conflicting views. Are we to believe that it is 'almost perfect' (ICM), or that it is 'a one-joke story, in need of considerable and major re-working' (NSWFTO)?

ICM

'A wonderful, funny, joyous screenplay that does just about everything right.'

'The characterisation is big yet realistic, the dialogue crackles, and the comic timing is incredible.'

'*Priscilla* opens with a bang and rarely flags . . . reminiscent of *City Slickers*, in that the pacing and jokes are that rapid fire.'

'There is little preaching about accepting alternative sexuality. It's an issue, but a secondary one dealt with swiftly.'

'The energy level *Priscilla* maintains is incredible. Every scene is a little gem, almost every joke laugh-out-loud.'

NSWFTO

'A shallow, predictable and not very funny formula comedy.'

'Lacking the depth in characterisation which might elevate it to something with greater dramatic and comedic impact.'

'The repetition of the same jokes over and over highlights the essential weakness of the script – its lack of dramatic action.'

'The script skates across the surface of more difficult issues, opting for a superficial comedic narrative.'

'One feels he is taking the safest story options, taking the path of least resistance.'

The Beginning

'Not since *La Cage Aux Folles* has a humorous film about gay men been so accessible. *Priscilla*, however, should prove a much bigger hit.'

'Fine as a 15-minute spot in a crowded gay bar after midnight, but a 90-minute feature film?'

In conclusion, I emphasise that when we have completed a location survey, we will make the dialogue sharper, the Outback detail more authentic, and some of the jokes more inventive, but what we cannot do is change the *nature* of the film, which is a piece of gaudy, mischievous entertainment about three people in collision with a sometimes hostile, always bewildering environment. The application is approved.

I continue to interview crew members, but I feel that we are losing momentum. Months after they have agreed to finance the film, PolyGram seem in no hurry to respond to the investment agreement, and my own impatience is augmented by that of their Australian co-financiers the FFC. There is no need for anything to take long or be complicated on a film like this, as PolyGram's film president Michael Kuhn emphasised at the time of their initial offer letter. 'If negotiations become too time consuming or bureaucratic,' he wrote, 'the whole thing is not worthwhile.'

To accommodate the delays prompted by Stephan's nervous exhaustion, by Paul Mercurio's restricted 'window' of availability, by Michael Hutchence's absence in Capri at an INXS summit conference about the group's future, and by the fact that if we have not started shooting by late

April we must wait until the end of August before the daylight hours become appreciably longer again, I draw up another revised schedule. There is no point in informing anyone of this until Stephan is back, Mercurio and Hutchence are signed and the financing contract is under way with PolyGram. News of postponement is a certain way of slowing down any process which requires acceleration.

The director is having a crisis of confidence. The two prospective leading actors are having a crisis of career direction. One of the financiers is having a crisis of indecision. The producer wishes he could have a crisis of anything but feels that all the best crises are taken.

Stephan returns, refreshed but not yet restored, and begins a regime of swimming, meditation, breathing exercises and general relaxation. These days we have so many methods of dealing with demons, so many incantations with which to keep rage, fear and loss at bay.

Although the picture is finally 'green lit' – at least, sufficiently to begin contract negotiations – we decide not to film at Sydney's annual Gay and Lesbian Mardi Gras, an event which, among other things, has helped to redefine drag. This gives Stephan the opportunity of attending as a participant instead. Dressed as a dog, at some moment well into the night he meets one of the investors' executives wearing a dress, so he drops down on all fours and starts barking at him.

The crew begins to converge. We need people of broad skills and tireless energy, and we are finding them. Colin Gibson and another art director, with one assistant, will be the entire art department, from finding a bus and redesigning it completely to decorating a country pub in the middle of the night before a shooting day. A confident and well-spoken drag queen called Strykermeyer offers to help create the drag make-up for each character, so we offer him two weeks' work and the title Executive Drag Consultant.

We are not, however, making any progress with the casting. As Hutchence and Mercurio recede into the oblivion of wishful thinking, we ask Bryan Brown, finding irresistible the prospect of one of Australia's quintessential 'blokes' in a frock, but he quickly turns down the offer. Stephan has a long conversation in Melbourne with the young actor Aden Young, who has a terrific screen presence but no apparent appetite or aptitude for comedy. A casting session for real drag queens results in such a notable number of no-shows that we call it off after a short time.

At this point we decide that it is finding the landscapes which will help to prompt new ideas about who could most effectively drive a bus through them. So we go to look for them.

The Location Survey

Priscilla

As Brian Breheny, Stephan and I approach the tiny aircraft which will fly us to Broken Hill, they are changing a tyre not much larger than that of a toy. It is an unpropitious start to a location survey which, with a few detours, will follow the route of the drag queens in the film. As well as giving us a measure of what is practicable, it will also benefit Stephan, who has written his Outback epic without ever having travelled west of the last vineyard in New South Wales.

Broken Hill is an Outback mining town just over 1100 km (687 miles) from Sydney. From the air it looks like an extended village of tin houses grouped around moribund silver, lead and zinc mines, but one of the reasons it has proved to be such a popular base for films over the past fifteen years – playing host to, among others, George Miller's *Mad Max 2* (*The Road Warrior*) and Russell Mulcahy's *Razorback* – is the great diversity of landscapes within driving distance. There are some signs of encroaching gentrification – art galleries, craft centres, a bad-pun hairdressing salon (Curl Up and Dye), a piss-elegant restaurant of the kind that lists mixed seafood dishes under titles like Neptune's Catch – but it remains mainly a good-natured down-to-earth border town, the last stop in western New South Wales before it gives way to the untamed heartland. Right now, after weeks of heavy summer rains, the surrounding countryside resembles a giant golf course, a rolling green Axminster carpet where there was once parched red earth.

Initially the Broken Hill Tourist Association, who provide transport and a succession of helpful guides, are the only people who know that the main characters in our movie are drag queens. With everybody else we confine ourselves to explaining that we are researching a film, and from the looks that Stephan's shorts attract in one of the first pubs we enter, it is probably just as well.

I also hint at the ambiguous sexuality of our protagonists to Mario, the Italian owner of the town's most extravagantly baroque hotel, Mario's Palace, a marvellous, hallucinatory, three-storey collision of kitsch which we want to use as a location. When I tell him that in the movie 'the wrong people wear the dresses' and that his hotel is 'drag queen heaven,' he smiles omnisciently, giving a persuasive impersonation of a man who has seen it all.

Mario is not popular in the town – it is said that his seventieth birthday party attracted very few guests – but we take to him immediately, and this is reinforced when we hear that the local health inspector has fined him for keeping a dead eagle in his fridge. His appeal that it was merely awaiting stuffing did not carry much weight after its proximity to the bacon rashers had been established.

While we find the perfect inland lake we need at nearby Menindee, and we are shown around an impressive variety of bar interiors – which prompts us to think that we may be able to shoot all the film's pub scenes in the same town – the only place we come across as unique in its eccentricity as Mario's is Stephens Creek, not far out of town on the road to Tibooburra. Approaching it, we see an eagle struggle across the road dragging a dead rabbit so large that the eagle is pecking away at it, trying to reduce enough of its bulk to be able to fly off with the rest. Several times the eagle tries, and fails, to get airborne. 'Big bird, bigger bunny,' says Stephan.

Stephens Creek is two buildings – a disused petrol pump with adjacent dwelling and a combined art gallery, tea room and owl barn which houses 'a collection of crafted owls', as well as numerous second-hand dolls and a 'trash and treasure' table. It is owned and run by a couple called Mitch and Val, who live there with a selection of century-old rockcakes, dozens of flies, a pile of laundry and their dog Bingo, who is so lethal he is kept locked up during our visit, all the while straining to escape his confinement so that he can jump at our throats and tear off our heads.

The fact that the characters in the film are so mismatched with the landscape means that we can also subvert familiar locations like the Pinnacles, Silverton and the look-out at Mundi Mundi Plain, the view from which – stretching to a horizon which seems so far away as to be on the other side of the world – will be the ideal place for our trio to realise the enormity of what they are about to travel through.

We rent a four-wheel drive and head west.

At its best, a location survey is more than a matter of aesthetics and logistics: it can make a film come to life in the imagination. There are so many hours of driving, so much concentrated time spent together, that ideas can spring out of word association alone. We decide we will shoot in Scope and really utilise the widescreen format, not concentrate the action in the centre of the frame in capitulation to the tyranny of video and television. We discuss comedy devices and decide that wipes and irises are the whoopee cushions of visual comedy. If we use wipes, Stephan concludes, it should be a giant pair of eyelashes blinking over the screen. We talk about road signs as punctuation marks and linking devices, with all the animals whose proximity such signs advertise – cows, camels, kangaroos, horses, wombats and so on – wearing dresses. And we amuse ourselves thinking up different titles for the film.

The full title – *The Adventures of Priscilla, Queen of the Desert* – still feels right because it captures the oblique comic-strip feel of the movie. It may even translate well, although the wordplay on 'queen' will be lost in other languages. Perhaps the only remaining detail that powerful actors and directors are unable to control is the title their film goes out under in foreign territories. *Housesitter*, for example, was called *A Blonde In My Soup* in Greece and *Lies Have Beautiful Legs* in Switzerland. *Home Alone* was released in France as *Mother, I Missed the Plane* and its sequel, accordingly, as *Mother, I Missed the Plane Again*. *The More Idiotic the Better* was the Brazilian title of *Wayne's World* and – best of all – *White Men Can't Jump* appeared in Spain as *White Men Don't Know How to Stick It In*. In Spain, where I was brought up, they never use a thumb tack if there is a nail and a sledgehammer around.

Then there are the running jokes. We decide that Mario – who says goodbye on roadside billboards for nearly an hour out of Broken Hill – is an early Bond villain in the avuncular style of Joseph Wiseman in *Dr No* or Gert Frobe in *From Russia With Love*, and that the reason he had an eagle in his fridge is that it was being implanted with a transmitter device broadcasting through the Telecom towers which punctuate the rolling Outback.

Apart from the Widelux camera he has brought with him so that the stills we take reflect the aspect ratio we will see in the movie, Brian has two special loves: the tracking road and the lucky shop. Whenever we see a good stretch of road on which to shoot an exterior of the bus, he automatically checks to see if there is a corresponding dirt track on which he can take a tracking vehicle. The lucky shop is his name for anywhere with betting facilities or slot machines, and it is his first port of call in each town we visit.

Hawker, in South Australia – to which we have driven along a track so extraordinary in its changes of landscape that we have been changing countries, from Switzerland to Scotland, every hour – does not have a lucky shop open on a Friday night, but it has a hotel with a pool table. Consistent with custom, Brian places some small change on the corner of the table, signifying his place in the queue to play. A gang of locals arrive and take over the table in a kind of group commando action, leaving him without a game. For a moment, he is prepared to take them all on in what would probably be a hideously bloody confrontation involving the entire bar, but Stephan dissuades him. Hawker, they decide, may be the home of the six-fingered washing-up glove.

I hear about this the following morning. I have missed the showdown by returning to my room to attempt to track down Tony Curtis, a casting idea we have had over dinner, at which Stephan has treated us to an account of a holiday visit made by him and his sister as children to their Uncle

Adrian's hog farm. One night they are woken by their mother and told to come and witness the miracle of birth. In their slippers and dressing gowns, they are taken to the resting place of a large sow and watch in wonderment as she gives birth to piglets. As the last one pops out, Uncle Adrian examines them. 'Shit,' he says, 'they're all runts.' Then he picks up the tiny piglets by their trotters and smashes them against a wall, to the horror of two screaming, traumatised youngsters. This, we agree, may have been his turning point.

From there we begin our trek north into the Conradian heart of darkness of the Flinders Ranges and the Oodnadatta track, the part of the journey where human sightings will be rare and luxuries, we feel sure, will become absurd sentimental memories. We have been advised, in particular, to look out for camels, the most dangerous of all desert animals at night on the road. Hit one with your vehicle at full speed and it will be the last time you make that mistake, or indeed any mistake.

The sealed road turns to dirt track again. There are abandoned, rusting cars with no doors or wheels, and dead animals – none of them camels – by the side of the road. It is a wonder that any animals at all can survive out here, and these have done so only to collide with one of the half-dozen motor vehicles that will pass this way on any day. We travel through and past places of myth, places that are part of the dreamscape of Australia: Marree, where the people we meet are doing mining surveys in a light aircraft; Lake Eyre, an enormous salt lake which retains sufficient moisture under its crusty edges to leave our vehicle stranded in the mud for ten minutes in which we could have become a tragic Outback case history; and

Beresford, a complete building in ruins, a desalination tower, a flowing water-hole and more galahs (small cockatoos) than it is possible to imagine in a single place.

By the time we reach William Creek in the late afternoon it is like a mirage in the dust. Here the flies, which have been increasing in abundance along the way, have practically taken over. When we drive out to take photographs of the desert sunset, they are an unavoidable mass: in the eyes and ears, up the nostrils, down the throat. We cannot open our mouths to speak, and it is fatal to use vowels, which require an increased aperture. Brian and I, in defiance, are attempting a ventriloquised conversation about great cinematography of the desert and I mention Vittorio Storaro's work on *The Sheltering Sky*. I forget that the enunciation of the word STO-RA-RO obliges the mouth to open three times. The flies just dive in, leaving the rest of the sentence lost in an insect-congested cough.

Back at the motel, after washing off all the dead insects, we sit outside in the twilight opposite what must be the most isolated phone booth in the world. Many miles away in the fading purple and pink, a road train lit up like a spaceship approaches slowly across the plains, leaving behind it a trail of dust like a whirlwind rising up into the sky. While Stephan calls London from the solar-powered booth, we watch in amazement as the huge illuminated truck comes closer, finally grinding to a deafening halt outside this shack by the side of the road which is our lodging for the night, covering us all in dust. Inside, we eat the finest steaks and drink the best red wine any of us can remember tasting, and we are struck by our good fortune. It is a very hot night but the flies have gone to sleep. Dreaming of the Swedish backpacker-girls in the adjacent camping ground, Brian sleeps on the hood of the jeep, then moves to the cool of the terrace floor. This is better than making movies.

William Creek, unfortunately, is not a place where we can make this one. By now it is apparent that, to shoot over these kinds of distances in the time we have, the film will need to be based out of as few places as possible along the way: probably Broken Hill, Coober Pedy (to which we are driving), Ayers Rock (if we can secure permission to film there) and Alice Springs. It will be a demanding schedule, but a necessary one if we are to convey a real sense of journey in the movie: the changes in the landscape are too dramatic for us to consider not travelling the whole way. We are not interested in the embalming pictorialism and cultural navel-gazing of Australian pictures of the 70s. We want the Outback to look like a lunar landscape, an alien environment to unnerve the drag queens, who will look like aliens in it. On the way to Coober Pedy, we stop at the Pink Roadhouse in Oodnadatta where a copy of the previous day's paper is on sale. It appears that the former chief of the FBI, who made it his life's work to investigate people's secrets, had one of his own. The headline reads J. EDGAR HOOVER, DRAG QUEEN. Here, on the edge of the Simpson Desert, it comes with the synchronous timing of a divine message.

Halfway down a track which links Oodnadatta and the Stuart Highway, we come across the Painted Desert. Although we are now accustomed to being in a state of wonder several times a day, this place is quite phenomenal. It is a perfect spot for Bernadette to do some

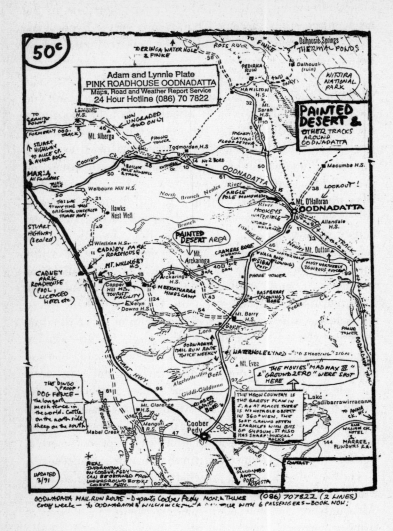

A customised guide to a lunar landscape

of her walkabout, when she sets out for help after the bus has broken down. We resolve that, however far we are from our Coober Pedy base, a skeletal crew will at some point make a detour to shoot it, with a stand-in if necessary. About an hour from Coober Pedy we break down. As the problem is connected with overheating, we look at the radiator. It is a frightful sight, a solid shield of flies and mosquitoes, a mass so densely indivisible that it prevents any liquid from circulating. We clean it sufficiently to struggle into town, where high-pressure hoses will finish the job.

Coober Pedy is opal country, where the mines in and around the town are not the only subterranean universe. There is another, stranger one which includes underground houses, an underground church and an underground hotel, the only place any of us have ever stayed in without ever having the slightest idea what time of day it is.

Roland, who has been recommended to us as someone who understands the dynamics of the town, is a Swiss chef living in a 'dugout', as underground houses are called in Coober Pedy. He is one of the few people who is not here to mine opals but to feed the gourmet tourists that pass through the town in ever increasing numbers, and those locals who have developed a taste for foccacia and capuccino. Despite a magnificent desert sunset outside, Roland is in his dugout sounding like Ingmar Bergman on a rainy day in Stockholm. I make a joke about the flies and the 'dragnets' we have been obliged to hang over our faces to prevent insects from making kamikaze dives into our mouths. 'I will not wear one,' he declares with sombre finality. 'I cannot look at the world through a net.'

Just outside the town we find three locations which perfectly reflect our idea of making the Australian desert resemble the topography of a bizarre planet. The Moon Plain – on which one can look in any direction and see no horizon, nothing but the sparkle of gypsum – is where we will shoot the sequence in which the young drag queen performs an aria perched in a giant silver shoe on the roof of the bus. Equally lunar in a different way is the Olympic mine, where we can film a campfire scene at night and the following morning's departure, its configuration of earth mounds by each mining shaft giving it an eerily galactic quality. Most arresting of all are the Breakaways which, seen at dawn, look sublimely like the islands in the sea they once were. The middle section of the film – the aftermath of the bus breakdown – will be shot there. To compensate for their lack of star power, independent films must have at least one unforgettable sequence which everyone talks about. *Priscilla*, I feel confident, will have several.

Driving north again, we discuss the music in the film. As well as the Shirley Bassey references, there are also Kylie Minogue jokes and a finale which involves her, or at least an impersonation of her. Because she is one of those figures whose topicality fluctuates according to whether or not she has recently reinvented herself, I feel that a pop act whose tacky qualities are more timeless would be better. When Abba emerge as one of these, I tell Stephan a story I once heard about an Abba fan on a cruise boat who entered a toilet that Agnetha was leaving and, finding one of her stools at the bottom of the bowl, bottled it and took it home. I also play 'I've Never Been To Me', by the American singer Charlene, which I first heard driving across Arizona with Andrena and nearly had to stop the car. We repeat it several times because the lyrics defy belief at a single hearing. ('Me' is a sort of comfort station of stabilising banality, to which one returns after having too much fun.) It is the kind of song which tends to be performed towards the end of wedding receptions by singers so enraptured by their own queasy sincerity that they virtually fellate the microphone. It also represents a genre of goofy melodrama that is raw meat to a drag queen. It is perfect, except it is on Motown Records and almost certainly unaffordable to us.

We also play movie scores, and the three of us have a competition to establish if we are able to hum the analogous main themes of Maurice Jarre's *Lawrence of Arabia* and John Barry's *Born Free* scores in sequence without transposing any notes between melody lines. At a roadhouse by the turn-off to the Painted Desert, we are having breakfast at a window table when we see a Japanese motorcyclist approaching a petrol pump. Despite the heat, he is wearing a large quilted jumpsuit, which makes him look like an oriental Michelin Man, and there is hardly an inch of him that is not covered in logos. He must be the first of a new species: the sponsored traveller. We name him Logoman and decide that he is probably working for Bond-villain Mario, helping to track his transmitter-implanted eagles around the country.

Since their residents are captives after sunset, none of the hotels are cheap at the resort village created to provide a base for Ayers Rock tourists. We stay at the cheapest, the one with the communal showers and bathrooms. The rock is a remarkable place – the Olgas, the neighbouring formation, even more so – and the red tint from its rusting iron oxide is spectacular at sunset. But I have seen it before, and I am mostly interested in returning with a film crew. We ask the resort manager whether it will be possible to film the rock on a long lens from one of the resort look-outs, which we could then match up with close-ups shot elsewhere. He says that it is, but that he has no wish to upset the good relationship which the resort enjoys with the local Aborigines and the Community Park Liaison Officer who protects their interests.

Following the earlier correspondence and rejection, we have drinks with the Community Park Liaison Officer, who brings along a member of the Mutitjulu Community and a civil servant from Melbourne. As the resort rooms are posted with notices from Aboriginal leaders requesting visitors not to supply alcohol to their people, I am a little surprised to find the one at our table drinking rum. He remains silent throughout the discussion. It turns out that the Community Park Liaison Officer knows quite a lot about Sydney drag queens, and mentions several of them by name, but he is politely, firmly resolute: we will not film there. Stephan is aggrieved, says so and leaves the table. There is really no more to be added.

Driving away from the rock towards Alice Springs, we are given the keys to the land surrounding Mount Connor by its owner. More overwhelming than the rock from a distance – Mount Connor truly resembles the 'helipad of the gods' which UFO enthusiasts have called Ayers Rock – it is less impressive close up and, crucially, it would be impossible for a film crew to climb.

In our exploration of Alice Springs and its outlying areas, we review numerous gaps and gorges, and – in a giant open-air version of a stage farce – collide with the

Swedish backpackers from William Creek, Logoman (forced by the heat into a lightweight version of the jumpsuit with duplicate logos) and Roland, who has mysteriously driven all the way from Coober Pedy to have dinner.

As the film is to be announced at the forthcoming Cannes Film Festival, we have decided that the most effective way of selling the movie, of capturing its tone, its essential joke of three people hilariously and tragically at odds with their environment, is through a single picture. In the absence of a cast, we have packed two dresses and a sequined swimsuit and brought them along with us with the idea of, somewhere along the way, slipping into the outfits, setting up the photograph and persuading a passing stranger to press the shutter. Finally, Stephan, Brian and I are struggling into our drag on a windy hill west of Alice Springs, looking out towards the horizon with the MacDonnell Ranges in the background. Stephan, in the simplest outfit, is enjoying himself tremendously; I am having a few difficulties with my heels and fishnet stockings; and Brian just looks like a cameraman in a wedding dress. A bewildered but fascinated backpacker friend of Roland's captures the moment.

Andrena, who has discovered that she is pregnant, meets us when we arrive at Sydney Airport the next day. The four of us sit on the beach at Watsons Bay as the sun sets, eating fish and chips and drinking champagne. We hope that the movie materialises, but in the meantime we are having the time of our lives.

The Launch

May 1993. We are leaving for the Cannes Film Festival to launch the picture – or at least to announce the prospect of its existence – without a single member of the cast in place. This means that we are straying close to the edge of the precipice, but there is a confidence in our stride which may keep us from falling over it.

If the role of the middle-aged transsexual Bernadette is to be played by the one permitted foreigner, our first choice is Tony Curtis, an engaging comic actor in the 50s and 60s, whose declining popularity and escalating substance abuse left him navigating a path through what turned out to be two-and-a-half decades of mediocrity. With the exception of Elia Kazan's *The Last Tycoon* and Nicolas Roeg's *Insignificance* – directors who knew how to exploit Curtis's ingratiating edginess – he has somehow managed to avoid appearing in an entirely watchable film since his spellbinding but short-lived change of gear as *The Boston Strangler* in 1968. (Reaching rock bottom in the early 80s, Curtis played Iago in a contemporary adaptation of *Othello*, 'based on the drama by William Shakespeare', called *Othello the Black Commando*, written and directed by, and starring Max H. Boulois. While acknowledging the competition presented by several of the works of Edward D. Wood Jr, this has the distinction of being perhaps the worst film ever made.)

Yet Curtis remains a star, an indelible memory, an exhilarating echo to anyone dreaming up a drag movie who has seen – as they must surely have – *Some Like It Hot*, still one of the quintessential film comedies. Our picture would enable him to go a stage further by playing a woman, rather than a reluctant transvestite with a weakness for Marilyn Monroe's body and Cary Grant's affectations.

The first exchange with a newly remarried Curtis has left Stephan completely infatuated. Weary of actors who not only require persuasion to wear dresses but reassurance that they will be permitted to project an air of competence in the film's musical numbers, he is relieved that Curtis cracked the code immediately. 'The thing I love about these guys,' said Curtis of the drag queens after reading the script, 'is that they have absolutely no talent.'

Unintimidated by the prospect of making a movie in the Australian desert as he approaches his sixty-eighth birthday, all he asks is not to be expected to sleep in a tent. He also has a winning way of concluding a conversation. As if possessed by the combined spirits of all the screenwriters of his much ridiculed early costume pictures, he lapses effortlessly into archaism. 'Excuse me Stephan,' he exclaims before hanging up, 'I must leave you now and return to my beautiful bride.'

There is an enthusiasm and complicity about his manner which continues in a series of calls and faxes – signed 'Hugs and Kisses, T.C.' – as he visits various American cities on his honeymoon. Then, mysteriously, we are unable to reach him. One senses a failure of nerve, as one often does with actors. He becomes a diminishing prospect, if not yet a completely lost one. He has gone to Europe, and his assistant makes familiarly evasive noises about whether our picture can now be made to fit his schedule. He really wants to do it, she says. Of course.

Stephan has finished a new draft of the script minutes before our departure from Sydney. I read it on the flight to Los Angeles. It is not particularly different from the old draft, but there are a number of additional jokes and characters inspired by our location survey.

I make some notes while he sleeps, mostly identifying what I consider to be banal or redundant lines. The script as a whole reads well. Unusually witty and unremittingly foul-mouthed, it has retained the originality of what made it worth making in the first place. There is something fundamentally mechanical about many screenplays because most of them are written to satisfy some threadbare, hand-me-down notion of what the marketplace wants. *Priscilla* just jumped out of Stephan's head, which is why neither the concept nor the characters have had a chance to be emasculated before they even reached the page.

In the departure lounge at Los Angeles airport, waiting to board the connecting flight to London, we discuss – far too loudly for some of our fellow passengers – whether or not one of the drag queens should threaten to rip off another's head and shit in her neck. The line stays, for the time being.

With the casting of Bernadette left in suspended animation, we concentrate on finding actors to play the other two leading roles. On arrival in London, we decide to reapproach Rupert Everett – who has retained a commendably ironic perspective on an earlier misunderstanding – for Tick. As he is already staying in the south of France, we arrange to meet him in Cannes later that week.

To play Adam, we pursue an idea we had about Jason Donovan, with whom we arrange to have lunch the following day. We are not sure if he is a sufficiently experienced actor to make Adam more than a mincing pastiche, but it will make intriguingly provocative casting in view of his recent history of litigation. He in turn can be conciliatory towards an audience which largely forsook him when he took legal action, and won, against the magazine *The Face* for suggesting he was gay.

We have another thought for Bernadette: John Cleese. A call is made to his agent: he is not interested.

So that there are no misunderstandings later – with PolyGram realising that the soundtrack to a picture they are half financing is being released by a rival record company (the terms of which agreement they would in any case need to approve) – I outline to various PolyGram executives and lawyers the deal we have with PWL Records. It is a pleasant but inconclusive encounter, and the two people present from the music division appear perceptibly underwhelmed by what I delude myself is the persuasive vigour of my pitch.

When we meet Jason Donovan and his manager at Il Siciliano, the kind of old-fashioned Soho Italian restaurant where it is a matter of policy not to take any notice of the famous, I realise that this is the third time I have approached him about appearing in a film. (I flew to the Gold Coast during the 1989 Australian pilots' strike to see him about *The Crossing* – when he felt unable to cancel a week of European record promotion to complete our mandatory ensemble rehearsal schedule – and to London in 1991 with the same director, George Ogilvie, to discuss another movie.) He is as charming as ever – equal parts surf yob and gracious young man – and he insists he is enthusiastic about playing the role, particularly as his appearance in *Rough Diamonds* – as, claims its synopsis, 'a cattle rancher and a superb guitarist' – seems to have fallen through. (The film is later made.)

Towards the end of the meal, at around the time he is telling us that he has never seen *Some Like It Hot*, a tall black woman runs into the restaurant, kisses him and rushes out. Suspecting a stunt, we speculate without success on where she came from and at whose prompting. We conclude that she was probably a drag queen spontaneously auditioning for the movie. By now, we are on drag queen alert: as far as we are concerned, any big-boned woman with a vocal register lower than alto could be one.

We invite Jason to join us in Cannes, where *Frauds* is screening in competition, and where he can also meet his possible co-star Rupert Everett and witness the process that makes the picture come together. It is beginning to look promising.

In the departure lounge at Heathrow, one can identify the various European nationalities by how they choose to kill time. The French and Italian talk among themselves. The Germans drink beer. The British read newspapers.

By the time we stand shuffling around the luggage carousel in Nice, the British have loosened up sufficiently to make small talk, punctuated by a kind of braying, mirthless laughter designed to obfuscate the steely resolve with which they are entering the Cannes Film Festival.

It is my tenth visit to Cannes and the first on which a car is scheduled to meet me at the airport. Inevitably, it is nowhere to be seen. After telephone calls to the publicists DDA – who represent *Priscilla's* sales agents, Manifesto – to JAC, the publicists who are handling *Frauds*, and to the festival office itself, nobody is prepared to accept responsibility for the car's absence. We take the bus.

As I frequently do on the first day, I have lunch on the beach with the producer Hercules Bellville, who is staying at the same hotel and whose unyielding (some would say insufferable) precision exceeds even my own. He also knows how to orchestrate an interesting social and business life more effectively than anybody else I have met. While envying his skill, and the fluency of his routine, I sometimes feel he has eliminated the possibility of the unexpected which those of us obliged to live more by our wits at Cannes encounter constantly. But I love the amused, rather patrician manner he and his colleagues like Jeremy Thomas and Bernardo Bertolucci project here, which once prompted Alan Parker to remark that when approaching their lunch table he always felt like the taxi driver who had come to collect them.

Our first meeting is with DDA and Manifesto on the terrace of the Grand Hotel. It is about publicity, which is the axis around which Cannes revolves: everything is to do with how one is perceived, and publicists are the architects of that perception. Unlike film markets – events rooted in traditional commerce which people attend to buy and sell movies rather than to admire them – Cannes' main currency is prestige not wealth. If you are considered important, and your self-esteem is unassailably resilient, the Byzantine layers of the place drop away along with its obstacles. People disregard your worst behaviour and sanctify your best.

We see the artwork for the announcement ad that Manifesto will take in the daily trade magazines. It is the photograph of Stephan, Brian and me on the hill outside Alice Springs, looking like Martians in frocks. I notice that my love handles have been airbrushed out by the designer, and I am complimented several times on my shapely legs.

The credits which accompany the photo are appropriately sparse. By the standards of festivals, where the promiscuous announcement of names rarely has much to do with reality, they are quite minimal. In being part of the official selection in competition with his first feature film, Stephan has been comprehensively ratified as an *auteur* (at Cannes, one hears of a film only in a context of who directed it), so it is original of him not to have proposed the now routine vanity credit 'A Stephan Elliott Film' above the title of *Priscilla*. This deplorable usurpation of the contributions of the other creative forces on a movie has spread like a bad rash in recent years, and doubtless Stephan's ego will eventually compel him to capitulate, but by then he may have earned his *auteur*ship.

Before, it was precisely that: something that people like Capra, Hitchcock and Hawks *earned*, and it became part of the marketing of the movies of a few truly distinctive directors. Hence, one does not begrudge Spielberg, Scorsese and DePalma a possessory credit (which they did not take on their early films) because their pictures are so emphatically made by them, but now every idiot with delusions and a combative agent demands it and, through the lap-dog acquiescence of studio executives, has rendered it meaningless. In view of this, it is revealing to enumerate those filmmakers who remain content to take simple directing credits: Francis Coppola, Woody Allen, Clint Eastwood, Sidney Lumet, (Dr) George Miller, Bruce Beresford, Phillip Noyce, Joe Dante, Steven Soderberg, Bill Forsyth, John Sayles, Jim McBride, Jonathan Kaplan, Steve Kloves. (Beresford once asked the Directors Guild of America if he could have the line 'a film by Bruce Beresford', which he had not requested, removed from the Sunset Strip billboard of *Crimes of the Heart*. Their response was that he was an unappreciative bastard for whom they had fought wars.)

After approving the *Priscilla* ad, we discuss the press release, which I propose to rewrite – the tone is too ingratiating, where I favour a kind of subtly aggrandising self-deprecation – and review the guest list for our launch lunch on Sunday at the Manifesto villa, which we will have an opportunity to inspect when we attend a party there later that day.

As the meeting ends, we notice that about two hundred yards off the Carlton Beach there is a giant inflatable Arnold Schwarzenegger, secured to a pontoon and holding what resembles a flaccid cucumber. We decide that it would be fun, and good publicity for the film, to swim out during the night and put an enormous dress on him.

Other than photographers – in whom Cannes brings out the pack-hunting predator – people tend to feign indifference to the famous before twilight. In the daytime, expressions of recognition are confined to the eyes. Rarely do heads actually turn, except to acknowledge the presence of a national idol like Alain Delon, or a global colossus like the inflatable Arnold Schwarzenegger, or a particularly striking woman dressed to emphasise, as Robert Mitchum once put it, her anatomical salients.

Or Rupert Everett. As he approaches our table on the Grand's terrace, heads turn. It may be his height, or his angularity, or his biker boots catching the morning light like some slow-motion reverie from Kenneth Anger's *Scorpio Rising*. It may even be because several films he has appeared in over the years have been in one or other festival category. Perhaps it is just the winning accessory of the very large dog that walks beside him. In any case, our quiet confidential chat is clearly going to be under review.

As he settles into his chair, Rupert – who has been told that he knows Stephan but is unable to remember from where – is relieved when he is given his bearings. In 1986 he appeared in the Australian film *The Right Hand Man* with Hugo Weaving, who is arriving in Cannes a few days later for the screening of *Frauds*, and who is interested in the same part as Rupert in *Priscilla*. Stephan was the second assistant director of *The Right Hand Man*, and Rupert is both amused and embarrassed by the prospect of being directed by someone from below stairs who may already have witnessed some of his worst behaviour.

More importantly, he loves the script. In the decade since he used to have sex with a female friend of mine in taxis, he has become, I am told, more overtly gay, but for us this is neither an asset nor a liability. He is palpably excited by the prospect of playing the most complex role in the film, and he has many entertaining and imaginative ideas about how he intends to approach it.

There is a problem, however. He is concerned about having Jason Donovan as his co-star. He couches this in the customary euphemisms, but the body language is unmistakably defiant. Perhaps the memory of the only other time he appeared in a film with pop stars (Bob Dylan and Fiona in Richard Marquand's barely released *Hearts of Fire*) is too grisly to consider repeating.

We sit firmly in our chairs and on the issue. Before making a conclusive offer, we insist that at least he meets Jason Donovan the following week to see if there is any combustion between them. He agrees, explaining he has a deadline for accepting the lead in an Italian porn movie – to be directed by the caliph of carnality, Tinto Brass – which he can probably extend until the last day of Cannes, but no later. Would he rather be a porn star or a drag star, we ask him as we part company and the people at the surrounding tables pretend to ignore us. We already know the answer, but we are not prepared to sacrifice another actor to hear it.

That evening we are reminded of the crucial nature of casting when we see David Thewlis's riveting performance in Mike Leigh's *Naked*. As Stephan and I approach the Palais, there is a tremendous clamour and I contemplate for a moment how the power of the director has escalated to a point where a respected but not especially renowned one can be given this kind of reception before his film has even been shown. Then a little way ahead we see Arnold Schwarzenegger. The rubber colossus has become a wax dummy, the smile melting under the lights, the arm waving on a slow pulley.

Making Priscilla

When we emerge from the screening, the inflatable Arnold has been deflated and tucked away for the night. I wonder how the wax Arnold responded to Leigh's harrowing drama set in a world that must have seemed a chilly stratosphere away. Before the film began, we are informed, the big man was escorted through the building and out of the back entrance into a waiting limousine, which disappeared silently into the night.

Relishing the prospect of finding a few feathers in the poached salmon, we have decided that there should be a strategically disruptive appearance by a drag queen during the *Priscilla* distributors' lunch at the Manifesto villa. Beyond the suffocating small talk, the trading of axioms as rigorously choreographed as dance steps, there is a place at Cannes for comic subversion, and we are determined to find it.

On our previous visit to the villa, while scanning the perimeter of the grounds we notice that beyond the swimming pool is a dip in the lawn, which rolls down the hill and obscures anyone crouching at the end of the garden. We imagine a drag queen in the midday sun, running in slow motion over the brow of the hill miming to Julie Andrews' 'The Sound Of Music', then molesting the guests as they attempt to take evasive action behind their *salades niçoises*.

We have no idea who is going to do this. Although Stephan has brought the sequined lime-green Esther Williams swimsuit and red tights he wore for the location photo – in the hope, one suspects, that his luggage might be searched at customs – we realise that, particularly at an *auteur*'s festival like Cannes, it ill befits a male director with a high-profile film being shown later in the week to dress up as a woman to entertain the prospective distributors of his next one. (It is difficult to picture, say, Jean-Luc Godard applying himself to this with much conviction.)

Dismissing the idea of encouraging the guests themselves to wear drag, we research the local transvestite scene. Our check list is unnegotiable: she must be able to speak English, be responsive to direction, be available for an hour of rehearsal the following morning and be lip-synchingly familiar with at least one of the songs Stephan will suggest. And, consonant with our budget, she must come cheaply.

Grant Lee has arrived in Cannes with a felicity of timing he may never exceed. He and Stephan return from a rapid round of the relevant clubs with only one marginal contender for what is, uniquely in this setting, a role nobody appears to want. Our putative star is demanding one thousand dollars for two hours' work, and with the Saturday night she has ahead of her it is unlikely that she will show up at the villa in a state to do much more than be sick over the distributors. There is only one solution at this late hour: Grant will go far beyond his brief as a trainee producer and become a drag queen, which we feebly attempt to convince him is what all producers fundamentally are.

Grant has not done this before. Having risen early to examine his outfit and practise miming to a Donna Summer song swiftly chosen from Stephan's cassette bag, he comes over for breakfast to discuss wigs and, more pressingly, where they might be found on a Sunday morning. The hotel concierge makes a number of calls, none of them successful. There is one last resort: a nearby joke shop, open on Sundays, which carries a limited selection of wigs among the stink bombs and the whoopee cushions. We select a hideous pink Afro, a refugee from some cross-dressing mutation of *Shaft*. We can hardly believe our luck.

Shortly after noon under a perfect Côte d'Azur sky, overlooking the bay still presided over by the inflatable Arnold Schwarzenegger with his flaccid cucumber, the turn-out is a little disappointing but the mood is buoyant. At some point between the asparagus tips and the raspberries, as I attempt to describe the movie to a reporter from *Film Français*, it happens: the music starts and Grant comes skipping up the hill, into view, in drag. There is no more effective way of concealing one's own embarrassment than to engender it in others, and as he struts towards the tables – unidentified by many of those present – Grant begins to fix his attention on the luckless individuals on whom he will linger a vital few seconds too long, leaving them shrinking from his attention. Miming to a disco song whose dance mix runs for what feels like several years, he threatens for a moment to lose his concentration, without which the whole pantomime will fall apart. But he struggles through to the end, running with a triumphant leap back down the hill and out of sight as the song fades. There is much applause, but we do not see deals being signed spontaneously on table napkins.

After a break, reinforcing our reputation as the festival's most tireless revellers, we return to the villa for somebody else's party. The entire day feels like a hallucination.

It is a few days later. There are numerous people with

whom to discuss business, but they will prove to be distracted encounters, escapist diversions leading to the moment in the late afternoon when Rupert Everett and Jason Donovan will finally meet.

Awaiting their arrival, we sit on the Grand's terrace under an awning, which strains under the weight of the rain that has punctuated the day. Rupert has driven in from his house in St Tropez, and we make desultory conversation with him as we scan the approach paths from our table, hoping for a sighting of Jason Donovan. A telephone call to Nice airport confirms that his plane arrived on time: we hope that he will have instructed the taxi driver to take him directly to where we are.

We try Jason's hotel, the Martinez, which appears to have come to a complete standstill. Elizabeth Taylor is presiding over a press conference for the film *And the Band Played On*, and the place is in the kind of disarray which in Cannes can only be prompted by the presence of a Hollywood evergreen on a slow day. The anecdotal fluency, which in the meantime has moved into overdrive, is just as rapidly declining. We begin to give up on his arrival. Instead, we make a dinner reservation and resolve to spend the intervening time tracking him down.

Another call to the Martinez reveals that he has checked in, then immediately checked out again. Someone in the search party has the number of a friend to whose house Jason may have driven. The friend says that he is on his way there but has not yet arrived. We leave a message with the location of the restaurant where we will meet him. Settling around the table under a cloud of early evening lassitude, we have completed the circle back to the nervous, vapid small talk with which we began the encounter. We all consider ourselves, as people in the film world invariably do, to be amusing company, but because we have met for a purpose to whose resolution we are moving no closer three hours later, the energy has evaporated.

The restaurant's telephone is perpetually occupied, so I return to the hotel to call Jason. As I look for the number, there is a ring in which the apologies are practically audible. He did arrive at the Martinez. Though no stranger to crowds, and unknown to most of the one which had gathered in and around the lobby, there was something menacing in the bustle and braying which completely unsettled him. So he left. I ask him if he is acquainted with Nathanael West's *The Day of the Locust*, whose climax contains perhaps the definitive account of crowd paranoia. He is not.

As he makes his way back into town, I return to the restaurant. Now *Stephan* has gone. A press screening of *Frauds* has just begun, and by now reluctant to miss it for a meeting that may never take place, he is on his way. In the escalating absurdity of the evening, we have found the actor but lost the director.

When Jason arrives, with a breathless and cheerfully self-deflating account of his rapid retreat from Cannes, the co-producer Michael Hamlyn and I attempt to steer the conversation towards Rupert Everett, who has become very quiet, studying his possible co-star with what can only be described as anthropological curiosity. When a kind of noncommittal civility represents the zenith of a discussion rather than its nadir, it is manifestly going nowhere. Which, despite the oceans of wine lubricating its course, is precisely where it goes.

The Launch

After midnight, I walk over to an empty Palais – which in the middle of the night resembles the shell of a Big Top after the circus has left town – for the ritual print rehearsal of *Frauds*, in preparation for its two screenings later that day. Stephan, Grant and I wait inside the stage door until the prosperous-looking entourage which accompanies *Much Ado About Nothing* – the day's main attraction with three screenings – has swished past us and out of the building.

My description of the dinner prompts in Stephan a passable impersonation of being perturbed, but tonight his mind, understandably, is on *Frauds*, and so for that matter is mine.

Thirty-six hours on, nobody is looking their best.

The shrill simulation of unerring self-confidence; the rooms full of colliding random atoms, desperate to be absorbed into a universe; the perpetual exposure to malicious egomaniacs, mean-spirited narcissists and calculator-toting gnomes; the no-taste hustlers who use their lack of imagination as a weapon, their solipsistic soundbites masquerading as conversation, their eyes turning cartwheels as their spineless venal schemes take hold.

All this, particularly when reinforced by alcohol and sleep deprivation, has a corrosive effect on the spirit, but it is the face which shows the evidence. Mine has a light application of Nivea. (When asked how he had retained his youthful appearance over the years of 70s' debauchery, Rod Stewart admitted that after a night's carousing and womanising he would always put Oil of Ulay on his face before retiring. The image of a drunken satyr in stack

heels daintily covering himself with cold cream at bedtime
has lingered with me ever since.)

We are recovering from the day of *Frauds*, which began
with an early-morning photo call at a merry-go-round near
the Palais and ended, for most, with an all-night party in
nearby La Napoule, at which Jason Donovan, wearing a
tuxedo and an expression of total bewilderment, had his
photograph taken with a very tall drag queen. (A believer
in choosing the moment to end an evening, I decided to
draw the curtains when a friend told me she had been
approached to produce a thriller in which the villain is a
microwave oven. It was a co-production, she explained,
and it was considered important to have a bad guy
everybody could recognise.)

By now, the word on *Frauds* is out: it has its supporters,
but it is generally not liked by the press, many of whom
are alienated by the unapologetic brashness of the
direction, and confused by the fact that a film so brightly
coloured could also be so black-hearted. Some ganged up
against it early in the festival, and the effect on the party-
line fence sitters could be felt in advance. Belittling the
movie as a lightweight vehicle for its star, they disregarded
a first-time director both in command of his medium and
taking risks with it: someone they should be championing.

We agree that the walk up the steps of the Palais with
the film's star Phil Collins – the crowd shouting his name
and the speaker system blaring Guy Gross's perfectly
deranged score – will remain one of life's outstanding
moments. When one of us says how comical it sounds to
hear hundreds of French people screaming *Pheel! Pheel!*,
the Frenchman in our midst observes, quite rightly, that
it is no funnier than hundreds of Americans all

mispronouncing Gerard Depardieu's name (*Gerarrd! Gerarrd!*) at the US premiere of *1492*.

We travel in several taxis, each with its own idiosyncratic way of getting lost, to a villa in the hills outside Cannes. Owned by Michael Hamlyn's father, it is the Versailles of rustic retreats, its grounds the size of a small country.

Much of what is being served at lunch beside the swimming pool was grown on these grounds, we are told, from which one could reasonably anticipate a spread consisting of most of the fruits, vegetables and wines of the south of France, supplementing a few roast suckling pigs from a neighbouring farm. Across the pool, the telephone rings.

Stephan is being courted by representatives of the three principal American show-business agencies, CAA, ICM and William Morris. The most effective courtship is being conducted by Bobbi Thompson of the William Morris Agency, whose tenacity is tempered with a playful intelligence; the most aggressive, by various CAA operatives. A few nights earlier, a couple of them, Perriers in hand, monitoring the bars for new clients (a recent feature of Cannes: the suits stay sober, the talent get drunk), came straight to the point with him outside some squalid watering hole. What exactly, they enquired, would it take to get him to sign with them? Sensing the absurdity of the moment, and regretting not having swum out to sabotage the now withdrawn inflatable Arnold Schwarzenegger, Stephan replied that the day he joined the agency, CAA's potentate Mike Ovitz would have to be wearing a dress. The operatives agreed unblinkingly.

It has travelled quickly like all good stories, and it has

reached a reporter from the *New Yorker*, who is calling to verify it. So while the other lunch guests eat olives and table-hop, Stephan finds himself phone in hand, pacing the perimeter of the pool, recalling the details of a half-forgotten encounter for the benefit of a journalist he will never meet.

Other than ourselves, the guests we have brought and the host family, there are only three people present who are not employees of PolyGram. One is Mario Van Peebles, the director and star of the black western *Posse*. The others are Rupert Everett and Jason Donovan.

Jason's style is collaborative – he talks to everyone around him without apparent regard for their status – while Rupert's is more conspiratorial, seeking out those whose view may carry some weight. Stephan, who is supposed to be orchestrating a conversation between them, is not doing so. Meanwhile, they do not speak to each other.

Although still exhibiting traces of yesterday's exhilaration – a director in competition at Cannes is king for a day – he is clearly exhausted, and it becomes apparent that this vital exchange, which could determine the future of *Priscilla*, is going to occur only in the most fragmented and rudimentary way.

He takes Rupert for a stroll through the olive grove and hears what he has to say. Then he wanders off with Jason for a few minutes, and afterwards I walk him around the orchard to find out what happened with both of them. The various configurations, and their concomitant by-play, are witnessed with some amusement by the PolyGram people, who are aware that what is taking place is a highly irregular casting session. Most bewildered of all is probably Mario Van Peebles, whose elected spot for a post-prandial snooze is next to the orchard path. From this position, he would hear every possible variation on the theme.

The decision is that there is no decision. We leave Cannes as we left Sydney: without a cast.

The Preparation

It is the choice of foreign actor, as is so often the case, which is going to be the decisive factor in whether the film is made, and Rupert Everett has decided to do the Italian movie. So we make lists.

It plainly needs to be someone affordable – eliminating the prospect of Bernadette being played by, say, Nick Nolte, whose usual salary is well over our total budget – but it is important we remember that some stars will reduce their fee if the role activates whatever vestigial sense of daring has not been eviscerated in becoming famous, and if they know that nobody else is being paid more. Otherwise, *Kiss of the Spider Woman* may never have been made, and William Hurt would not have won an Oscar.

There are hardly any overseas contenders to play Adam, and in any case it is the kind of part in which it would be simpler and more appropriate to cast a young Australian actor. Of the few we discuss, Jaye Davidson from *The Crying Game* is antithetical to our casting philosophy – in two words, against type – as, for the same reasons, is Julian Clary. The third British suggestion is Prince Edward, who I decide can wait until we do *Priscilla – the Panto*, with Merv Hughes as Tick and Richard Attenborough as Bernadette.

If we had been making this as a studio picture thirty

years earlier, we would have offered the leading roles to people like Burt Lancaster, Lee Marvin and Steve McQueen, the kind of testosterone-saturated actors who are now an endangered if not extinct species. As it is an independently financed movie in the 90s, the American actors we consider for Tick include Kyle McLachlan, Rob Lowe and Matthew Broderick. The British prospects are Colin Firth, Rupert Graves and Cary Elwes; the Australian ones, Hugo Weaving and Sam Neill. Increasingly, Hugo Weaving feels like the right choice. Often cast as anally retentive adults, he is really a naughty boy, a performer of tremendous range and sensitivity who also understands Stephan's spirit perfectly. But we have to cast *around* the foreign actor, in whatever role he is to play, and it is when free-associating between names for Bernadette that our conversations move into a truly demented realm. Starting with some regard for reality by enumerating a few British actors, young lions of the 60s, who might now bring a poignant dimension to an old girl in a frock (Peter O'Toole, Richard Harris, Albert Finney, Alan Bates), we deteriorate into cross-media madness (Cliff Richard, Clive James, Dudley Moore).

We approach Colin Firth, who was outstanding opposite Rupert Everett in *Another Country*. Firth is acceptable casting to PolyGram, and although I am wearying of these protracted and unconsummated serial courtships, Stephan has an encouraging lunch with him which ends with a declaration of mutual interest in doing the movie together.

For reasons to do with the end of June also being the end of the Australian financial year, we have a very short time in which to sign the financing agreements with the various parties. And as Colin Firth's name will need to be included as a preapproved and contracted 'essential element', we have no time for the time-consuming two-steps of the negotiating dance floor. It seems that the imminence of an offer to appear in *Priscilla* prompts actors' agents in London to leave their offices and put themselves out of contact for several days. Firth's is no exception. Meanwhile, Stephan's now likely American agents William Morris send us their own lists, on which all the casting suggestions for the transsexual Bernadette – Julie Andrews, Ann-Margret, Lily Tomlin and others – are already women. This at least brings a completely new perspective to resolving our problem.

Stephan's feet have barely touched Sydney ground again when we hear that Colin Firth has changed his mind. There is a personal difficulty to which he must attend, and a corresponding reluctance to make himself available for the two months in which we require him for rehearsals and filming. It is not the only crisis we have, but it is the one which aggravates all the other ones.

With nine days to go until the execution deadline of the various agreements, I am feverishly trying to co-ordinate them all, and to provide the information required to satisfy everyone concerned. Although I have made the situation clear to them, I am not sure PolyGram fully understand that if the contracts are not signed during the last week of June, the FFC will withdraw. This is not the kind of spurious threat favoured by brinkmanship negotiators; it is an irrevocable fact. Cashflow must have begun by the end of the financial year for the rest of the funding to be implemented and, of course, the cashflow cannot begin until the contracts have been signed.

The acceleration towards the chequered flag begins. In

the course of a single day I speak to six lawyers representing different interests and attempt to mobilise a collective effort. Then they all speak to each other. We have secured an increase in the final budget, which allows us to spend a greater proportion of time on the road, to build four days of travel into the schedule, and to enable a small increment in the salaries of the crew, many of whom have still not been found. Although we are offering a rare combination of adventure and profit points as compensation for low wages, several people we respect pay lip service to the principle then walk away.

But there will be no film at all without an approved cast, and no chance of finding one if we do not keep moving forward. Everybody is too far down the track to want to pull out, so we agree to sign subject to casting being approved prior to investor cashflow. There is still one month before the start of pre-production, and Latent Image will spend its own money until then. The contracts are executed – and the signature pages circulated by fax – fifteen minutes before the close of business on the day of the deadline.

On the flight to Los Angeles – from where he will continue directly to London – Stephan encounters Paul Mercurio again. As the star of a successful movie on his way to see *Pretty Woman* director Garry Marshall about a leading role in Marshall's next picture *Exit to Eden*, Mercurio is travelling at the front of the plane. As the director of a low-budget comedy with no cast in place and no money in the bank, Stephan is travelling at the back. Undeterred by the gulf between their circumstances, and aware that they are trapped in the air together, Stephan has a final, purposeful shot. All Mercurio can do to avoid the issue is to run behind the first-class curtain and call a member of the cabin staff to provide security. However alluring it may seem to work with an American director on a studio picture, Stephan tells him, *Priscilla* will be the film to stretch him as an actor and, more importantly, will be much more fun to make. Mercurio says he is still interested, and will consider his options after meeting Marshall.

By the time Stephan has landed in London, more names are flying around: the American actors John Cusack and Eric Stoltz for Tick and – a brilliant piece of deranged lateral thinking – either Superman (Christopher Reeve) or Captain Kirk (William Shatner) as Bernadette.

The people he has really come to see, however, are Rupert Graves for Tick and Tim Curry for Bernadette. I am not in favour of Graves, still preferring Hugo Weaving both as an actor and as a grounding agent for Stephan when he is trying to direct the actors – covered in flies, with their make-up running – in the middle of nowhere. But Curry, who is in Vienna playing Cardinal Richelieu in *The Three Musketeers*, is an interesting choice. We know each other from having studied drama together at university, although I have only seen him a few times since *The Rocky Horror Show* and its consequent movie version made him a celebrity. The fact that he has never eclipsed the transvestite role which launched his career makes him approach *Priscilla* with equal measures of curiosity and caution.

Then it happens. It is not quite Paul on the road to Damascus, and I am unable to recall which one of us first brings up the name, but it is an indication of how congested our minds have become that we have neglected the perfect actor to play Bernadette: Terence Stamp.

He fits all our criteria. Although for the past sixteen years – punctuated by the occasional idiosyncratic detour with directors like Peter Brook, Stephen Frears and Pilar Miro – he has been playing supporting roles, usually villains, in big-budget studio pictures, he has retained his star aura, his looks and his heterosexual charge, which will make his transformation into a transsexual all the more startling. Adding resonance to this, and blurring the lines in a way that will make them more interesting, is the sexually ambiguous air he carried in some of his 60s' roles, notably in Ustinov's *Billy Budd* (which earned him an Oscar nomination in his first film) and Pasolini's *Theorem*.

While aware of the need for a change of gear in his life, Stamp's first response to reading the script is a wary one. He has never appeared in a comedy, unless one counts his star-billed but essentially supporting turn in Joseph Losey's ill-fated *Modesty Blaise*. He has never been in a musical. And he has never played a woman. On the other hand, he has been to Australia – accompanying Jean Shrimpton to the Melbourne Cup in 1965 – and he did not enjoy it, to the extent that he has left a standing instruction to his agent over the years not to consider film offers from there. But his agent is also Michael Hamlyn's assistant's brother's agent, so this one has slipped through the net. Michael himself is on holiday in the south of France, and is spending so much time on the phone to London he may as well have stayed behind.

Stephan calls after his meeting with Stamp, who has impressed him. 'He fills up the room as soon as he walks into it,' says Stephan, 'then he starts leaving you space.'

Stamp is naturally anxious about his hair, make-up and wardrobe if he is to succeed in a role so hazardous that failure, he feels sure, will lead to ridicule. He is also concerned about his co-star. Not about the two other leading actors with whom he will spend the majority of his screen time, but about who will play Bob, the Outback garage mechanic who develops an attachment to Bernadette, with whom he ends up, as the script so poetically calls it, 'playing hide the sausage'.

Aware that the other actors have to be Australian, Stamp suggests Bill Hunter, with whom he appeared in Stephen Frears' *The Hit* nine years earlier. They have barely seen each other since then, but Stamp remembers him with fondness and feels that an existing rapport between himself and the person playing Bob will bring a vital conviction to their scenes together. I call Bill Hunter's agent and inform her that Terence Stamp has specifically requested him as his 'love interest' in the film. When she speaks to him, Hunter laughs in disbelief and says he will accept the part without even reading the script.

By the end of the following day, Stamp has agreed to travel to a country he dislikes, Australia, to play a role that unnerves him, a woman, in a a genre he has never attempted, the comedy-musical.

The faxes from Terence Stamp begin to arrive the day after Stephan's return. Several of them are about his feet, which fortunately have not become cold. First an enquiry about what kind of shoes will he be wearing in the film, as he is going to have a practice pair made by Anello and Davide. Then his tailor's measurements, with illustrations in the style of a vintage menswear catalogue. Finally, immaculately detailed drawings of his right foot, then his left – each faxed foot transmitted at a different time – revealing one bottom instep marginally smaller than the other.

With Stamp on board, we can start the engines. We will cast Hugo Weaving as Tick if he can find a way of attending our rehearsals as well as fulfilling his contract with the Melbourne Theatre Company to appear in *Much Ado About Nothing* in Melbourne and Hobart. Stephan travels to Melbourne to screen test Guy Pearce – a young actor best known for his long residency in the Australian soap opera *Neighbours* – for the role of Adam. As we are unable to afford a rehearsal room in which to film, it is done in the local offices of the FFC.

The crew is coming together in consonance. We find our first assistant director in Stuart Freeman, who began his film career as a third assistant in England with the Boulting Brothers in 1956, seven years before Stephan was born. His work as an assistant director, location manager, second-unit director and production manager spans all the 60s and 70s, and I deduce from his resumé that he travelled to New Zealand as the assistant director of Mike Newell's *Bad Blood* in 1981 and has stayed in the Antipodes ever since. He has worked on movies in all our planned locations, but his current employment in Western Australia will prevent him from joining us until two weeks into pre-production. It is a risk we will have to take. We persuade Owen Paterson – the production designer of *Bliss*, who has forsaken films for commercials in recent years – to work with Colin Gibson in the minimal art department. And Sue Seeary, who I assumed was contentedly developing her own material while producing a documentary, turns out to be available and interested in production-managing the picture. It is turning out exactly the way we wanted: a combination of accomplished professionals doing or returning favours, and inexperienced but skilled newcomers with a desire to prove themselves.

Some of them are already working, even as we walk the tightrope that determines if the film will exist. The costume designers Lizzy Gardiner and Tim Chappel have been in New York, shopping for wardrobe at a drag supermarket called Peggy's Mardi Gras. It is the kind of place where they have to let you in. You ring the bell next to a substantial steel door, somebody upstairs presses a buzzer and you go up in an elevator. The supermarket itself is bright and busy, with muzak and cheery lighting, and three transsexuals in aqua tracksuits as store assistants. Their purchases include silicone breasts at $800 a pair, foam buttocks resembling pitta bread to build up Bernadette's hips, and the black dress she wears in the funeral scene. A number of languidly absorbed men in suits, ties and wedding rings are feeling up the shoes.

When they return, Lizzy and Tim are also instrumental in persuading Stephan that Guy Pearce is the perfect Adam. His screen test is outstanding, but there is something in Stephan that worries about the role lapsing into caricature, to which he feels a 'straight' actor will eventually resort in order to sustain a role of such queeny flamboyance. I disagree entirely, feeling that what all the parts need are good actors, regardless of sexuality. We are not making a documentary.

Although he is becoming more confident as each

successive stage is completed, Stephan is still going through occasional moments of terror. One night he drives over to our apartment to say he is no longer sure he can make the film. I tell him that it is not the kind of project on which anyone is staking their professional lives. It is a small, diversionary, one-of-a-kind movie that will restore a sense of adventure to everyone involved. If it is not funny, it will simply evaporate, and after falling off his horse with *Frauds* he should – to stretch the equine metaphor to breaking point – get back in the saddle again for a low-stakes race. Citing one of our favourite films by a man who never directed another, I remind him that he is not Charles Laughton and that this is not *The Night of the Hunter*.

A week before the start of pre-production, I arrange a Saturday morning meeting at the Latent Image offices so that the heads of departments can be briefed by Stephan in a way which may be informative for everybody. A few of the group know him well, more have a passing familiarity, a few have never met him at all. I have been warned by Grant earlier in the morning that, for various personal reasons, Stephan is not feeling well and may not show up at all. But he is persuaded, and he does.

From experience and reputation, these people think of Stephan as a buoyant, iconoclastic, amusement arcade of a personality, so when this bleary, unshaven, clearly upset man walks into the room they are confused. He certainly does not resemble the writer-director of a funny road movie. Perhaps we have gathered them for a purpose, to reveal that the dates are the same but the project has changed, that we are instead remaking Tarkovsky's *The Sacrifice* in the Outback.

67

Making Priscilla

A bus has arrived outside to audition for the role of
Priscilla, so the moment is not permitted to develop past
the first few minutes of what shows perturbing signs of
developing into a group therapy session. By the time we
return – after surveying the vehicle from all angles and
with every technical consideration in mind – the mood has
lightened considerably, and a sense of purpose is restored.
It is Stephan's last moment of irresolution. From now on,
his sense of mission becomes unswerving. Having come
close to losing it, he has decided to find it, and this time
to keep it.

When we move into our pre-production premises at the
Sydney Showground, everything begins to accelerate.
    Lizzy and Tim have already begun making costumes in
a glass garret above my office, designing to a background
of likely soundtrack songs. Hugo will wear Tim's own
silver-sequined knitted dress for the film's solo opening
number, and they have also decided that Hugo's frock for
the drag queens' walkabout in Broken Hill will be made
entirely out of credit cards. As none of the credit card
companies will give us clearance, and since nobody owns
the copyright on the use of thongs, Lizzy and Tim come
up with an even better idea: a thong dress, with tiny thongs
for earrings and Chanel straps on a thong handbag.
Without a cent to waste, they call Tim's mother who works
in the shoe department at the Warringah Mall branch of
K-Mart and, through her, receive a 15 per cent staff
discount on several dozen pink and orange thongs.
    Lizzy's boyfriend, the television director Andrew Saw,
is in the office one evening, and I tell him of the difficulty
we have in finding a place striking enough to stand in for

Ayers Rock, in the likely event that we continue to be refused filming permission. He suggests we try somewhere called Kings Canyon, north-east of Ayers Rock and west of Alice Springs. It is spectacular-looking, he says, and well disposed to filming, with nearby hotel and backpacker accommodation. He encourages us to include it on our imminent location surveys, which we are doing in the aberrant way which everything on this movie seems to demand. Stephan, Grant and Colin Gibson will fly to Alice Springs and Kings Canyon, scanning locations in both places, then rent a car and drive to Coober Pedy and Broken Hill, where they will do likewise. When they arrive in Broken Hill, they will meet up with Sue Seeary, Stuart Freeman and the location and unit manager Rick Kornaat, who after briefing will take the same vehicle back in the opposite direction, confirming the places along the way that Stephan has approved and ensuring that they work from a practical point of view. As the link between the two groups of explorers, Grant travels both ways.

I make a final attempt to secure an Ayers Rock filming permit and receive a response from the Australian Conservation Agency. I am not sure what their connection is with the other organisations we have already encountered, but the message is clearer than ever: the rock portrayed as it is, even if the film is a comedy, is 'offensive to the traditional owners'. The not-so-traditional owners of the resort village, who have been considering allowing us to film a long shot, decide to reinforce the decision and also decline.

The single most dominant characteristic of film pre-production is the remarkable amount of overlapping activity. Movies are passed around: Terence Stamp pictures, musicals, cross-dressing films. Stephan is just off the plane from Alice Springs, with a favourable report on Kings Canyon, when he takes another one to Melbourne to rehearse Hugo and Guy – whose schedule on the TV series *The Man From Snowy River* prevents travel to Sydney – together. The wardrobe fittings are a great success: Hugo runs around the hotel in a white wedding dress, which he refuses to take off. A 42-page fax arrives from a choreographer looking for a job. Our office machine does not include a cutting facility, so it emerges as a single, continuous piece of paper, stretching the entire length of the office. We employ somebody else.

Even with an ally at PolyGram music publishing in Sydney, and a composer friend who tracks down fifteen out-of-copyright numbers for various uses, the song clearances are still proving frustratingly difficult at this late stage, but I brighten when I hear that PolyGram has bought Motown Records: it may mean that we can use Charlene's 'I've Never Been To Me' after all. There is still a great deal of procedural tedium, hair-splitting, teeth-grinding paperwork connected with the completion bond, the insurances, the frequency and amounts of the cash drawdowns, and the maximum balance permitted in our account before PolyGram will send us any more. It seems to me pointless to have an approved cash drawdown schedule unless we can count on the money being in the bank on the appropriate day every week.

A title search report – which one is obliged to do as part of the film's insurance arrangements – reveals that someone once published a book called *Lady Hester Stanhope: Queen of the Desert* and that there is a fresh vegetable company in the United States called Desert

Queen. Neither is likely to sue, I feel. The Marx Brothers once received a letter from the legal department at Warner Bros cautioning them against including the word 'Casablanca' in their title *A Night in Casablanca* because it infringed, claimed the lawyer, Warner's exclusive rights to its use in a title. In his reply Groucho pointed out that the Marx Brothers had been brothers for longer than the Warner Brothers, so he could just as legitimately insist that the Warners stop using the word 'Brothers'.

Then there is Priscilla herself. We have finally found the bus, and in a neighbouring hangar a team of destroyers and designers begin to transform her. The sound of drills, soldering irons and hammers is a distant echo for two days. On one of them, I am leaving the office late one evening when I hear a different sound: it is Tim Chappel shaping emu heads out of a block of polystyrene with a sabre saw.

Terence Stamp – in linen under a Panama hat – arrives on flight QF4 from Honolulu on August 26, eighteen days before we begin shooting. An experienced traveller, he has been resting in the sun after an American press junket for the film *The Real McCoy*, in which he plays another of those sullen bad guys from whom *Priscilla* will at least provide some kind of relief. He spent much of the 70s seeing the world, taking the occasional low-key European film role to subsidise his odyssey, before returning to the screen, memorably, as the villainous General Zod in *Superman* and *Superman 2*.

He has arrived in Sydney with no body hair, or at least very little. After a body wax, each of his nipple hairs was pulled out with tweezers. He has also completed a course, intended to put him in touch with his feminine side, in which one of the challenges was to do something you feared in front of the others. His was to sing in public, so he did it, a kind of karaoke for the psyche. He is reading Jan Morris's book *Conundrum*, which includes a description of a sex change operation that leaves even the most imperturbable reader gagging for air.

On his second night in town, still jet-lagged and disorientated, Terence is walking from the city-centre cinema complexes back to his hotel and realises after a while that he has no idea where he is going. Under the giant Coca Cola sign at Kings Cross – fortuitously only five minutes from his destination – he sees a large fellow in a tuxedo standing alone, so he approaches him for directions. 'I'm lost,' says Terence. The big man is clearly a philosopher. 'Aren't we all, mate,' he replies. 'No,' says Terence, 'you don't understand. I'm really lost.' By now, there is a flicker of recognition. 'Here,' he asks, 'weren't you General Zod in *Superman*?'

Wigs, shoes and costume fittings, make-up tests, dance rehearsals: we are in overdrive now. Hugo is flying up from Melbourne every day for rehearsals in frocks, and going back on the afternoon plane to do Shakespeare in tights. Guy is on horseback in moleskins in the Victorian mountains one moment, and mincing around in heels in the Sydney Showground the next. I feel that Terence is a little shocked by his 'show' costumes, which are a universe away from the natural fibres and Holly Golightly elegance he probably had in mind. Lizzy emerges from the wardrobe department one afternoon, tears of laughter running down her face, and asks Stephan to approve a costume. He enters to find Terence looking like a very glum emu indeed, although he is extremely fetching in the blonde wig on which he insisted - Stephan wanted him as a brunette – and he is receiving special coaching in walking and deportment from a 'tranny trainer'.

We meet the tranny trainer one night at a hotel in Newtown, where the cabaret includes three members of the crowd baring their buttocks on stage through a toilet-seat-shaped hole in a screen. Afterwards one has to match the blokes with the bottoms. Then there is a polywaffle-sucking competition, which involves six men and three sticks of chocolate-coated candy, and we hope that nobody will try to force us up on to the stage. But this is nothing. There is still a very special outing to come before the cameras turn.

By the time I arrive at the club called DCM, the night is well under way.

The movement order for the three actors has been precision tuned. Meet at Hugo Weaving's house, where the make-up department will prepare them for the wardrobe department, who will dress them. Go to a bar called Gilligan's for a few loosening drinks with Bill Hunter, who has brought a friend along to protect the 'girls' from any unwelcome harassment. Walk down the street to DCM, the club to which a few days earlier we brought Terence and Hugo to meet a couple of drag queens. Now they *are* a couple of drag queens.

The third one, Guy Pearce, is nowhere to be seen. It turns out that he is on the other side of the room, abusing everyone and demanding that drinks be bought for him as a reward for his unpleasantness. It is striking what an effect the disguise of drag is having on their personalities.

It makes Guy flirtatious, combative and loud. It makes Terence withdrawn and watchful ('Hello sailor,' he greets me warily with his back to the wall, looking like a fallen woman in a 50s' melodrama.) It makes Hugo extraordinarily trashy. Wearing an ash-blonde wig which always looks as if it may be dislodged by his succession of strange postures, he behaves like some drunken trollop in a country-and-western bar, the kind that gets more maudlin as the night progresses and tries to drape herself around the wrong kind of strangers. Right now he is draping himself around most of the table as his head – which has been wobbling forward in the manner of those people who fall asleep in a sitting position in cinemas and trains – finally connects with the glass top, as if the force of gravity were unable to raise it again. There are few signs of life other than a tapping index finger which would be keeping time to the music if it were about 100 beats-per-minute slower. Eventually, he is taking up so much room that we move him to the floor under the table, where we leave him inert as Guy becomes more obnoxious and Terence more austerely ladylike. They are working out their characters in the course of the night, defining in public their predominant characteristics in the movie.

Eventually it is time to leave. I escort Terence, in his black cocktail dress and high heels, down the steep staircase to the street. He is still finding his drag legs, and there is some relief as he tears off his shoes as we stand on the pavement. 'These heels are fucking *killing* me,' he says with exasperation, for a moment looking and sounding like some unholy alliance of Mamie Van Doren and Reggie Kray. The taxi driver takes us back to Hugo's house, where I ask him to wait. When we emerge ten minutes later, the driver's face drops. Having dropped off a man and a woman, he is now picking up two men, one of whom left his cab as a woman. While Hugo makes his way back hanging out of Stephan's car vomiting into the night wind, I drop Terence off at the Sebel Townhouse.

As he left the hotel earlier in the evening, he took the precaution of explaining to the receptionist that he was going out for the night to research a role and that, consequently he may return wearing a dress. 'Yeah,' she said with a dismissive shrug, 'that's what they all say.'

The second assistant director has measles. In sequence, these are among the six most dreaded words a producer can hear on the eve of a film shoot.

Although we have immediately found a replacement, her scheduling duties have required her to mix with all the cast and crew. Those who have had contact with her at the most contagious stage a few days earlier – contact is defined as being within a two-foot radius of the infected person, so this means practically everybody – have been recommended a couple of preventative gamma globulin shots, which are administered in a small tent in the base camp we have set up in a small car park close to the location. For the first three days, we are filming in a Sydney bar and the adjacent streets.

In what has been an unfortunate weekend generally, the art department runner's vehicle was broken into and the camera truck was involved in two accidents: one in which the driver misjudged the truck's height and ran into an awning, the other in which he misjudged its width and sideswiped a parked car.

Michael Hamlyn has arrived in Sydney and realises, in a way I have been unable to convey to him on the phone, the extent of our difficulties in finalising song clearances through PolyGram in London. One of the obstacles is Abba, and for various reasons connected with the renegotiation of their contract, PolyGram are now suggesting that we approach them ourselves, or come up with somebody else. I have explained that because the three main characters make a living out of miming to other people's records, the production and costume design have to reflect the kind of repertoire that they favour, and that Stephan has storyboarded and rehearsed the main musical numbers around this. Because of these problems, the rather lugubrious Abba song with which we were going to open the film has by now been superseded, to my undisguised delight, by Charlene's 'I've Never Been To Me', but the staging of the final number 'Mamma Mia' is scheduled for the second day and simply cannot be substituted at this stage. As we already have Abba costumes, Abba wigs, Abba choreography and Abba running jokes in the script, it follows that it must be Abba.

We require dull skies for our first day and they materialise. We are filming the arrival of the bus Priscilla (soon to be referred to on the daily call-sheets, with no definite article, as Bus Priscilla), its champagne christening and subsequent departure from Sydney, with Rebel Penfold-Russell as the departing sponsored runner Logowoman (a mutation of the Logoman we encountered on the location survey, and literally a running joke), with as many partying extras as we can find. After dark, we begin the scene in which Tick walks through the rain to call Bernadette. The intention is to convey the impression of a punishing city they would want to leave, and the conditions certainly make those of us behind the camera want to leave it. Although we have a rain machine to control the volume of water, when it is switched off it keeps raining anyway.

Making Priscilla

On the second day, we shoot the first and last scenes in the movie. Hugo Weaving's myth-making Charlene will provide the main titles sequence, his performance shot from angles which will allow the relevant names to be superimposed over both strategically empty spaces and particular objects, such as a mirrorball and a pool table. As we do a semi-circular track around him in close-up, Hugo's lip-synching is perfect, his concentration complete. Moving on, we introduce an afternoon crowd of a hundred or so to be rowdily demonstrative during a performance of 'Mamma Mia', with Hugo done up as Frida from Abba in her perm phase and Guy as Agnetha. It is an awkward few hours: spotlights keep failing and a tracking shot through the crowd is time-consuming to orchestrate, but the song never fails to exhilarate. As we are finishing, Hugo's breasts start falling down, and he remarks on this. Stephan has kept the camera rolling and orders him to smile, which provides us with the freeze-frame that leads into the end titles. We work two hours overtime, by doing so completing some of the most important footage in the film, which will eventually represent over six minutes of screen time.

Three days of interiors later, I am, as they say, ready for my close-up. After a show-stopping appearance as an insurance executive in *Frauds*, Stephan has asked me to play the minister at the burial of Bernadette's young lover Trumpet. For my first clerical cameo, I bring along the twenty-third psalm and a pair of sunglasses, requiring only a cassock from the wardrobe department to complete my authentically ecclesiastical persona.

It is a cloudless spring day of rising heat, a climate inconsonant with my outfit and, particularly, with that of the mourners, a small group of Sydney's most illustrious drag queens. Stephan and Tim Chappel have been up for most of the night, concluding it at a place called the Taxi Club where they offered a number of drag queens $100 for showing up later that morning in a graveyard in Newtown dressed in black. In the middle of the scene, it becomes too overwhelming for one called Mogadonna. So she lifts up her veil, excuses herself and discharges her breakfast all over a gravestone.

In the cemetery, at least there are no snakes. There are many at West Head – part of a national park at the northern end of Sydney – where we are filming the first scenes after they leave the city on board Bus Priscilla, still travelling through lush countryside. We are warned about the presence of a variety of highly toxic ones – the death adder, the tiger snake, the brown snake, the red-bellied black snake – and the detailed first aid instructions are a testament to the proximity not only of snakes but of Australia's oldest killer, the funnel-web spider.

Nobody is thinking much about snakes or spiders because two rigs – invented by a coalition of the camera, electrical and art departments – whose success will in many respects determine the practicability of the shoot, are being put into practice for the first time as the bus drives repeatedly up and down the road. One is an interior tracking rig for the bus, which will allow the camera to be moved inside the vehicle without the need for hand-held photography. The other is a lighting rig positioned on scaffolding outside the bus in order to light the interior. The erection and demolition of this, according to whether or not the exterior of the bus is in shot, will become a feature of the scheduling. To our relief, both work.

One of the extras from the cemetery scene, a renowned Sydney disciplinarian called Madam Lash who sported a rubber dress on the day, has turned up at the location just before the dinner break, when it is impossible to escape her. She intends – she announces to me and to anybody who cares to listen – to paint Terence Stamp in drag in the Outback, and she will not accept rejection easily. Her timing is far from perfect. My only interest is in building the kind of momentum which constantly overcomes obstacles, and I see any distraction – in the form of press, photographers or portrait painters – as the enemy of that objective. As well as being an intrusion, which will lead to a closed set from now on, this is also not the right evening to approach Terence. He has seen some raw footage on film – although we are transferring to tape for editing, we print selected takes whenever we are concerned about lighting or focus – and he is not pleased with his appearance. Brian would light him a little more flatteringly, glamorously even, but Stephan keeps whispering in his ear that he wants to see every wrinkle.

After an interval of nearly nineteen years, I am about to become a father again. I decide that while the cast and crew travel to Broken Hill on Thursday – and for those driving the trucks, part of Friday – I will miss the Friday afternoon and Saturday filming and, if the baby has not made an appearance by Monday, take the morning plane to Broken Hill. The airline timetable in both directions does not leave any latitude for impulsive travel, but it will become even more difficult to return from Coober Pedy, the next town along the route, so I will fly back to Sydney the following weekend.

The Shoot

I call the office in Broken Hill on Friday afternoon. Everybody has arrived, although the people who flew found that most of their luggage was removed from the plane, to be sent on later through Adelaide, and those who drove Bus Priscilla and the make-up truck both had to stop to change tyres. The latter vehicle broke down as well, arriving late when it needed to be early to do the 'girls" make-up for the walk around town.

At the final birth class in a series which Andrena and I have been attending, the instructor does a demonstration on what resembles a small hot water bottle sheathed in a child's cardigan. She refers to it as 'a knitted uterus', an object so kitsch I consider how effective it might look hanging from Bus Priscilla's rear-view mirror like a pair of furry dice.

It is my responsibility to ensure that every aspect of the film works at its optimum, and to engender a support structure around Stephan that permits him to concentrate on getting the best results. On set I express my point of view to him, but it is understood that he can take it or leave it. Although I am not above pulling the plug at the natural end of a working day, a director should feel completely secure during a film shoot, and while I do not delude myself that I am useful all the time, part of taking responsibility is to be present, so that is where I like to be.

Sue Seeary and the production co-ordinator Esther Rodewald – both friends of Stephan's for some years, who understand his whims without surrendering to them – are running a remarkable two-person production office. In a strange echo of our first impression of it earlier in the year, Broken Hill is hosting its first golf tournament that weekend. Apart from the crew located at Mario's Motel – a functional rooming house behind his baroque Palace, where we will be filming – everybody is engaged in a perpetual shuffle of hotels, and the production office is leading the way by changing almost daily. It will not be the last accomodation crisis.

On arrival, cigar still unlit, I watch the footage which was shot in my absence. Although the drag walkabout in Broken Hill will cut together well, and Hugo's long confessional around the campfire has been beautifully performed in a single set-up with only one cutaway, the film's first real piece of wide-open-spaces bravura – and therefore, in terms of moments achieved so far, the highlight – is an extended shot of the trio at dusk, rising up on the crane towards the sunset on the Mundi Mundi Plain using a 25mm lens which makes the three figures look as if they are taking their first steps towards falling off the edge of the world.

All filming in the 'magic hour' at sunset, by its very nature involves a race against the fading light, and we accelerate towards Menindee Lake to maximise the time available. However prepared one is, those last few minutes before dark are always over too quickly. In this scene, the three principals and Bob, who is by now travelling with them, run into a lake they have found, to their astonishment, in the middle of nowhere. There will be a flash of Terence's emerging wet torso, so while the water-filled condoms he usually wears make an acceptably busty contour in clothing, for this shot we require the real breasts of a Scandinavian backpacker body double, one of six women who auditioned their bosoms for Stephan in the production office.

The Shoot

We finish just as the light goes and drive back to Broken Hill to our next engagement. Stephan, Guntis Sics the sound recordist and I have a date with a local pianist in his loungeroom to record a version of 'I Don't Care If The Sun Don't Shine' that can be played through most of the following day's bar scene.

It is the first of two successive days beset with difficulties in Broken Hill bars. At Mario's — where we shoot the sequence in which our hero(in)es have a confrontation with a tough Outback woman Shirl whom Bernadette goes on to beat in a drinking contest — extras keep looking at the camera, sabotaging otherwise good takes, and the smoke keeps dispersing, but if there is an open door nobody can find it. June Marie Bennett, who plays Shirl, was the star of the Broken Hill stage production of *Hello Dolly* and, while she does not much like her outfit of singlet and bra, her particular difficulty is remembering her lines, which Terence writes on a piece of paper, pointing to each one with his fingernail as she delivers it. Stephan and the first assistant director Stuart Freeman are well on their way to a showdown. As a former assistant director, Stephan is rigorously exacting and more splenetic than most if he considers the job is not being done to his satisfaction. In turn, Stuart has worked on more films than the rest of the crew combined and does not relish displays of impatience bordering on public admonitions from an exasperated young director, however talented. They are not getting the best out of each other, and by now are finding it difficult to communicate. Although the customary procedure under these circumstances is to dismiss the less essential person, I will not fire Stuart Freeman. While he works at a slower

83

pace than Stephan would like – and Stephan is invariably ahead of most crew members – he is a seasoned professional whose experience will, I feel, help to navigate us through the difficult days ahead. But the problem needs to be worked through, and I sympathise with both of them. I talk to Stuart after we have finished shooting for the evening, and tell him the areas in which we need to see a change of approach. I am confident we can make it work. We *have* to.

The following day a hot northerly wind blows up a whirlwind of mineral dust around the All Nations Hotel, and everybody is very edgy. The 'girls' are inside a trailer being fitted with ridiculous cheerleader outfits of crystal organza and polyester, which will keep falling down as the day goes on. They are to perform a brief routine on the bar-top to Peaches 'n' Herb's 'Shake Your Groove Thing', interrupted by the arrival of Bob's Filipino wife Cynthia, who after a few drinks tends to show up in the pub wearing a catsuit with a zip strategically positioned to permit the firing of ping-pong balls out of her vagina. Julia Cortez, the actress who plays Cynthia so outstandingly, has brought her own costume, a garment so awesome Lizzy and Tim would have had difficulty in eclipsing it.

The extremes of weather are affecting not only people's nerves but the practical aspects of filming. A suddenly ferocious wind tears the 'blacks' which block out the light into the bar, and it takes half an hour to secure them again. Later, there is a generator breakdown, which forces a hundred already uncomfortable extras to be disagreeably confined with nothing to do except get drunk. More uncomfortable than any of them is Terence. This is the day on which a fundamentally serious movie actor has

been obliged to come to terms with the fact that he is
standing on the counter of an Australian bar, dressed in
one of Lizzy's and Tim's most absurd creations, being
leered at by miners as he tries – repeatedly, and for much
of the day – to lip-synch, dance in heels and tear off his
pigtails to a forgotten disco song. (Terence will later
identify this as the moment when he went through the fear
barrier and capitulated to the absurdity of the film. It was
certainly a long way from William Wyler and *The
Collector*.)

We finish late, to a fanfare of torrential rain. When I
fly out of Broken Hill the following afternoon, floods have
closed many roads, confining us to interiors, and the plane
goes through an electrical storm of an intensity which
prompts me to wonder if I will survive to witness the birth
of my child.

The baby, unconcerned with *Priscilla*'s schedule, is not
quite ready to emerge. Andrena goes for a swim, hopeful
that exercise may help to engender some movement,
perhaps even symbolically break the waters, but nothing
happens. Somebody tells me that vodka martinis are a
little known but highly effective labour inducer, so I call
a bar renowned for the potency of its cocktails and ask if
they would be prepared to make four 'to go' and pour them
into an empty vodka bottle. I collect them in the rain
which has followed the flight all the way from Broken Hill
and take them home. Laughter might also help, and as I
am running a little short of it, we watch Stanley Kubrick's
distressingly hilarious *Dr Strangelove*, whose concluding
explosion might set off a few internal associations. So, the
checklist is complete: exercise, vodka martinis, film
comedy. And an audio tape from Stephan, as he likes the

idea of his future godchild being born to a succession of cheesy pop songs and nauseating show tunes.

It works. Thirty-two hours later, Rachel Maria Priscilla Clark makes her first appearance about thirty minutes after the mother and midwife have duetted to Helen Reddy's uniquely awful 'I Am Woman'.

The infatuation with my baby daughter is such that I do not call Broken Hill until the following day, just before everybody drives to Coober Pedy. The sun has come out; Bingo the homicidal dog of Stephens Creek has gone over the edge (there is a picture of him pressed up against a car window straining to kill someone, the flash revealing a canine Hannibal Lecter); a service station in which we were going to film has been replaced because the Christian fundamentalist owners of the land did not want a bus with the graffitti AIDS FUCKERS GO HOME in its courtyard; and a unit assistant has had a shattering experience with a glass partition. A convivial group of crew members with acoustic guitars were relaxing over an after-work singalong of 'Here Comes The Sun' when he suddenly came crashing through from next door, shards of glass hanging from every part of him. In an appearance fraught with the danger of severed arteries, he has escaped with a few cuts. Stryker, whom we have taken on full-time in the make-up department, was particularly impressed. 'Now *that's* a drag queen entrance,' he exclaimed approvingly, as people cleared the room.

In Coober Pedy, they will be joined by the original second assistant director, who has finally recovered in time for the twentieth day of the shoot. By not arriving until the twenty-first day – in a tiny plane from Adelaide

Me, Julia Cortez, Stephan Elliott. Ping-pong balls will soon fly. ELISE LOCKWOOD

Frida and Agnetha, unexpectedly reincarnated as Hugo Weaving and Guy Pearce. ELISE LOCKWOOD

Accustomed to being in a state of wonder several times a day...

Grant Lee, going far beyond his brief, stands in as a drag queen: Cannes 1993.

... we survey the Painted Desert. BRIAN BREHENY

**Stephan, Michael Hamlyn and me in Cannes
before the start, the inflatable Arnold
Schwarzenegger just out of view.** RICHARD BLANSHARD

**In a Sydney cemetery in shades.
My ecclesiastical cameo.** ELISE LOCKWOOD

Hugo in the Breakaways: a drag natural.
ELISE LOCKWOOD

**Life on a low-budget musical. When the actor
changes outfits...** ELISE LOCKWOOD

... the producer stands in. MICHAEL HAMLYN

Guy "does" Verdi: a new view of the Outback.
ELISE LOCKWOOD

**"Gumby" costumes by firelight: 52 set-ups
by dawn.** ELISE LOCKWOOD

A few hours later, these drag queens will be airlifted by helicopter. ELISE LOCKWOOD

Leaving Alice in a lavender bus: Mark Holmes and Guy. ELISE LOCKWOOD

Guy, Terence and Hugo: the first moment of awe. ELISE LOCKWOOD

The Sydney Opera House in drag.
ELISE LOCKWOOD

blown around in the sky like a tin can – I miss the filming of Felicia on top of the bus, her silver train billowing across the Moon Plain. The scene was shot by Brian – who is the camera operator as well as the director of photography – in a 15-knot gale on a tracking vehicle with a crane, but he is caught up in the excitement of the movement and the moment. It is only when he climbs a scaffolding tower for the long shot that he begins to feel queasy.

We have travelled from floods to hot desert winds, which are blowing across the Breakaways as I drive up. We are filming the bus breakdown scenes, in which the realisation that they are stranded prompts very different responses from the characters: Bernadette walks off to find rescue, Tick rehearses a new number and Adam paints the bus lavender. By doing so, he turns it into bus number four. There have been various versions of the bus: the one Adam buys; the one in which they leave Sydney, with the shoe and the drag interior; the same bus with added graffiti; and the lavender edition, which is the fourth. At one stage, there is a fifth – half lavender, half silver – which the second unit shoots. The bus is a wonderful sight, but what really triggers the primal memory of what made me produce the film is finally seeing Hugo in his lime-green dress working up a dance routine for 'I Will Survive' in perfect isolation on top of the salt-and-pepper hills.

It has been a long Saturday after what has been, for many reasons, an unusually eventful week. When we finish, Marike the caterer prepares dinner for everyone in one of the hotel kitchens, and we eat it in the shadow of the big widescreen television we install wherever we go to watch the tape transfers of our negative sent back by the laboratory. Everybody drinks too much and misbehaves in the knowledge that they have no obligations the next day. I make an early evening date with Stephan and Brian to show them two sections of Sergio Leone's *Once Upon A Time in The West* on video: the very long, nearly mute, famously inventive first scene, and the shooting of the rancher by Henry Fonda and his raincoat-clad henchman, with its wonderful transitions from foreboding to awareness to sudden death. Stephan and Brian have enough ideas of their own to make several movies out of *Priscilla*, but I want them to see this to remind them of the power of extreme close-ups in widescreen movies, which by favouring the panoramic view often exclude those supercharged, pore-examining shots of eyes and noses above perspiring upper lips.

We have been told about a film called *To Wong Foo, Thanks For Everything, Julie Newmar*, whose title is exactly as long as ours and several times as ridiculous. It is being made by Amblin Entertainment, the production company owned by Steven Spielberg, and for a moment we are troubled to hear that it is about three drag queens driving across America. When we read the script, it is evident that we have nothing to worry about. The tone of *To Wong Foo* is quite different from ours, its characters Pollyannas in dresses who straddle the main demographics of the United States: a white, a black, a Latino. With star casting it may be more successful than ours commercially, although on a cost-to-return ratio I doubt it: our entire costume budget would probably buy one of their stars' evening gowns. More importantly, it is still some time away from shooting.

There are flies everywhere. They make the flies at

William Creek who nearly choked me to death on the location survey seem benign. And there is the sensitive question of the art director Colin Gibson's underwear, or rather the absence of it. Several of the crew, referring to him as 'sausage pants', request he wear some layer of camouflage so that as he scurries about the set the outline of his member is not, as they put it, 'in their faces'. It seems that even under the most primitive conditions, decorum prevails. Characteristically, Colin ignores everything except what he is doing at the time.

The second-unit camera has been damaged after falling off a shelf in a moving truck, and the replacement camera arrives from Sydney missing a door. At this distance, in this isolation, it is impossible to obtain equipment quickly, which means we do not have the second camera we need on the twenty-fourth day of the shoot, when we are scheduled to spend the entire night filming the scene around the Aboriginal campfire. So we hastily replace it with the night scene at the drive-in, where Felicia shows up on drugs and in drag, and the ensuing chase through the street to a wreckers' yard, where a group of miners are about to do some damage to him. There are two immediate consequences of the change: the Aboriginal actor Alan Dargin, who is contracted to appear in Tasmania two nights later, will need a charter flight to take him to Adelaide to make the connection after the following night's campfire shoot, and the hilarious soft-core porn film we have shot, with several friends and a large dog, for background use in the drive-in scene has not yet arrived. (In any event, the 16mm projector's 'throw' does not work, the drive-in's original 35mm one having fallen into disrepair.)

Making Priscilla

Michael Hamlyn's assistant Clare Wise has gone around Coober Pedy and found as many Aboriginal extras as are prepared to spend what promises to be a cold night outside with us in a dip just off the track to William Creek, a location found at the eleventh hour, closer to town than the Breakaways, which we are unable to use, yet providing seamless continuity.

Although they will be surpassed when we do the climb in Kings Canyon, and again during the dance number in Alice Springs, the costumes look extraordinary, the prodigious ingenuity once more compensating for the absence of money. Inspired by the TV cartoon character Gumby – who looks like a long eraser that has been split in half – the costumes are body-fitted stretch jumpsuits topped with illuminated headdresses of fruit and flowers and flaring down from the knee to accommodate footwear that suggests, in outline under the material, skis made out of foam rubber.

It is an exacting night, yet despite constant retakes for focus and delays prompted by repairs to the fragile costumes – Terence takes a tumble at one point, which is just discernible in the final dissolve of the scene in the finished film – we somehow manage 52 camera set-ups, the last five in a flurry of activity – a race for the dark, as it were – as the dawn light spreads first across the horizon then up into the morning sky, revealing a cold grey day of gathering storm clouds. We drive Alan Dargin to the deserted runway at Coober Pedy airport, whose single building opens only when a scheduled flight is due. Awaiting the arrival of the charter, exhilaration has given way to exhaustion and we sit silently, with only the sound of the wind. Ten minutes pass. Twenty.

Thirty. Phone calls are made, but the plane can only radio out: it is not possible to check its position. Eventually, it arrives, delayed by the strong winds. In order to finish the scene before taking Alan to the airport, there has not been sufficient time to remove the glitter and glue from his hair, so he climbs into the plane looking like an extra from *Superfly* who has strayed into a drag queen's make-up bag. In this film there is glitter everywhere. In a long-shot on a 300mm lens in the middle of nowhere, Stephan still catches tiny sparkles on the actors' faces.

By the time I get back, the hotel has opened the bar for us, and as it begins to pour outside, so do we, happy that the night is over with what promises to be impressive results. Terence, with whom I spent a while standing around the campfire discussing his 1968 western *Blue* – in which he simultaneously took over Robert Redford's role and Elvis Presley's dressing room at Paramount – joins us briefly, astonished that our first instinct is not to go to bed. It is our second, and it can come later.

The torrential rain increases our schedule by a day. Coober Pedy – a desert town with an annual rainfall so negligible it is hardly worth recording – is awash during our final days there, so we have to film when we can, in the knowledge that trucks will sometimes become bogged in the mud. The Olympic Mine, where our shoot extends into the night after two successive days of rain, is full of mining shafts which we mark off with bright yellow tape, in dread of the echo of plummeting screams.

It is becoming less like *Lawrence of Arabia* and more like *Apocalypse Now*. During the 750 km (468 mile) drive from Coober Pedy to Kings Canyon – some of it along a dirt track which has been further eroded by the bad weather – we begin to feel we are on a journey up river to find Colonel Kurtz. The production office car, with Sue and Esther inside it, rolls over at some speed, leaving them physically unhurt but severely shaken. The crane hits a stone, damaging the transmission and requiring emergency repair work. Several vehicles have tyre blow-outs including our own, which Terence has driven like a champion, even if his false nails – much admired by the ladies at the supermarket in Coober Pedy – rather inhibit the effectiveness of his tyre changing. He learned to drive on unpaved roads when he lived in Ibiza, and it is a skill which has not deserted him. While Grant sleeps in the back seat, we talk. His performance is by degrees revealing itself to be remarkable – the restraint and the flaws of movement somehow enhancing the vulnerability of the character – and I admire his nerve, which he knows he might lose if he views the daily footage.

The rain, which has followed our trajectory from South Australia and across the Northern Territory border, has enveloped Kings Canyon when we awake the next day. We shoot a couple of interiors scheduled for Alice Springs, one of them the scene in which Bob knocks on Bernadette's door with the rescued flowers. Bob is the straight man who falls in love with a transsexual, so in many respects this is the riskiest scene in the film: it challenges assumptions about transsexuals as asexual beings, and about whether the Australian counterpart of the Marlboro Man could ever fall for one.

We must have three sunny days in Kings Canyon if we are to complete our work there, and fortunately we get them. On the first, we shoot several bus scenes before it becomes bogged down and then, late in the afternoon after a two-and-a-half hour make-up and wardrobe change, we do the chopper shot of the three drag queens standing on top of the canyon. It is a glorious sight: a blowing blur of feathered headdresses as they approach the helicopter, which deposits them near the edge of the highest escarpment before returning to collect Stephan, Brian and the camera.

On the second, we film the preceding montage, the climb itself. So we ascend, under a pitiless sun and cloudless skies, carrying equipment as we go up the rock face. By now we are sufficiently relaxed to have two journalists, a photographer and a television camera crew in tow. We are delivered lunch by the helicopter, which has already filmed Tim Chappel – sitting in for the climbing Guy Pearce – in the shoe on top of Bus Priscilla, a Verdi reprise that leaves a trail of pink and yellow smoke hanging in the Outback air. As the light begins to fade over the canyon, the safety officer decides that we will soon be stranded in the dark at high altitude. So he orders an emergency evacuation: eight trips by two helicopters to bring the cast and crew off the top of Kings Canyon and back to base camp, an airlift completed just before nightfall. One can almost hear 'Ride of the Valkyries' mixed in with the sound of chopper blades.

The third is a less exciting test of nerves: a hot, slow, monotonous day, with a long road journey to make at the end. The sound mixing equipment is blown over by a gust of wind, and a replacement will need to be sent to Alice Springs. When we finally finish shortly after six o'clock, I offer drivers the option of staying the night in Kings

Canyon or driving through to Alice Springs, six hours away by truck, some of the journey along the same dirt track on which the accident happened. If they have any doubts, I encourage them to stay. If they prefer to reach Alice that night, I encourage them to drive. On a location movie spanning three-and-a-half thousand kilometres, there is only one precept: *keep moving*.

My car has been appropriated by a group which left earlier, so I travel in the four-wheel drive with Stephan, Brian and Lizzy. We take a short cut involving an even longer stretch of dirt track. It is a shocking mess and we have to stop to wipe mud off the windscreen after every flooded hole we pass through. To amuse ourselves, each of us relates some incident in our childhood that was particularly traumatic for ourselves or our parents. Lizzy – with her tales of a Shetland pony, a turtle on a rope and a baby kangaroo that died of diarrhoea after eating too many cornflakes – outshines us all, although it is Brian who leaves us all startled and silent in poignant contemplation: his father, exasperated that his son was still using a dummy at the age of four, took it out of his mouth, threw it up in the air and shot it to pieces.

Arriving famished in an Alice Springs restaurant where last orders are being taken, I am nearly lynched by an alliance of those who set out early and have been worrying for hours about our welfare, those who have lost friends in road accidents after long shooting days, and those who have experienced for themselves the state of the particular track that we travelled on. There is a kind of suppressed hysteria in the air, and I am too weary and dusty to respond to it. I still feel that I made the correct decision, and both Stephan and Stuart Freeman have reinforced it.

The Shoot

We are not children and nobody has been under obligation.

We take a table in the hotel bar adjacent to the front entrance, and begin ticking off names. Terence arrives with a vehicle completely encased in mud after driving the flooded shorter route, his smile bespeaking an adventurer's gratification. The trucks that set out begin to trickle in and the luxury of the hotel, after our living conditions for the past four weeks, has an immediately palliative effect. A couple have called in to say they will pull over and sleep, completing their journey at sun-up. By three-thirty in the morning everyone who was expected has arrived.

We are filming by the following afternoon, already aware that we will require an additional day in the final week, which means that Bill Hunter — after a haircut, a shave and a change of wardrobe — will still be able to start work on *Muriel's Wedding* the following Monday. If, that is, we can find the condoms which have been performing as Bernadette's breasts and are now missing. A call goes out. They are returned by the people who wanted to use them for sex and restored to their proper function.

After dark, we are working on the campfire scene in which the four travellers talk before Bernadette is left with Bob. The location is a dry creek bed outside Alice Springs and although there appear to be no people or traffic in the area, we can hear noise. The safety officer and unit assistants investigate the source and at the other end of the creek find a trio of rowdy locals with a utility full of shit, beer and guns. The shit they collect in country areas with no plumbing, the beer is to help them become even more drunk and the guns make them dangerous. They are also very large – dwarfing even the biggest of our platoon – and, in the case of one, completely naked. They have no idea that a couple of hundred yards away are a cross-dressed man playing a cross-gendered one (Terence Stamp), an Australian national treasure (Bill Hunter) being romanced by him, and a lavender bus full of frocks. But they can see lights and the nude one starts to lurch towards them before being brought down by a rugby tackle. The explanation that we need quiet because we are shooting a film only confuses him more, since the word 'shooting' makes him think of the guns he has in his vehicle, which is stuck in the sand. At one point he decides he wants to have sex with our quietly spoken Bus Priscilla driver and starts to charge him rectally. For a while, it is like *Carry On Deliverance*.

We must maintain a swift work rate during our week in Alice Springs, but staying in a resort hotel is proving to be a restorative and the only really big scene to come is the staging of the main production number 'Finally' – four minutes of song, four costume and make-up changes – which we are filming over two days, the second an abbreviated one. I drive out to the airport to collect the choreographer. All the passengers on the same flight pass through the terminal and there is no sign of him. Then I see him, in the distance, hobbling towards me on crutches. At first I think it may be a joke, like a sound recordist turning up with a giant hearing aid, but he is conspicuously in difficulty and in pain. The actors are no less so at the sight of him: their big moment will be rehearsed under the guidance of a dance instructor who is no longer able to show them what to do.

The Shoot

Having postponed his wedding twice to accommodate our changing schedule, Guntis Sics the sound recordist has left to get married. We send him a telegram from Bus Priscilla, whose luggage compartment, sometimes doubling as Adam's bedroom, was his base for sound recording while travelling. If a message could purr, this one does. 'You spent so much time around me, beside me and inside me,' it begins, 'and you know all my secret places. No one has ever got quite that sound out of me before.' His replacement is going to experience a demanding couple of days constantly re-cueing the dance number, but the wardrobe and make-up department will have the most difficult time of all.

Lizzy and Tim have designed the four costumes to represent a kind of deranged cross-section of Australiana: flowers, emus, lizards and architecture. The last of these is represented by outfits that initially look like something Marie-Antoinette might wear to a kitchen tea but reveal themselves in the final frame to represent the Sydney Opera House. Owen Paterson has created a simple, extraordinarily effective backdrop, broadly evoking Aboriginal art, which is transformed by changes in colour.

As I am present on set every moment of the first day, pushing the pace to complete the scene in the time allocated, I feel bound to co-operate when Stephan decides to do a shot from behind the trio on stage wearing their flowers outfits while the actors themselves are changing into emus. I stand in for Bernadette, Grant abandons the second unit to deputise as Mitzi and the choreographer's boyfriend impersonates Felicia, and although the resultant shot ends up on screen for only a couple of seconds, it gives variety to the montage, demonstrates our enthusiastic dancing style and reveals again the legs that elicited all those compliments from PolyGram's sales agents.

The next day is simpler in routines, more complicated in costuming. The lizard outfits have frill necks which have to materialise dramatically if it is to be worthwhile having them materialise at all. For longer than we can bear, they remain flaccid. The opera house outfits are full of fibreglass kite rods, and they too cause problems, but not as many as the extension cords coming out of the actor's wigs, the lights in which are controlled manually by Lizzy. We finish only a few minutes over schedule. It is a colossal achievement.

After that everything feels like the end of term. We finally have the crew photo taken, in drag: blokes with facial hair and chest fur wearing dresses and wigs next to a lavender bus in the midday sun. Everybody knows that they will never have a team-spirit adventure like this again.

With all we have been through, the last shot – a bus interior, with several of us shaking the bus to simulate movement – is chronically anti-climactic. But we look up at the sky and there is one more. An enormous orange full moon – a Scorpio moon, says Terence – is rising over a nearby hill, and the second-unit cameraman, who has returned from an afternoon at the races in Alice Springs $1500 richer, is despatched at high speed towards it.

By the time he reaches it, it has gone white. But we use it anyway. This is a low-budget movie.

The Cut

QUEEN OF THE DESERT

December 15. There is no experience to compare with flying into Los Angeles at night, but this morning the city in clear winter daylight has an extraordinary lustre.

Three days of torrential rain have washed away the smog, and the details within the limitless sweep and sprawl are thrown into startling relief from the air: the geometric configuration of roads, the snow-capped mountain ranges, the punctuating azure of swimming pools that resemble tiny windows in the earth. Jack Kerouac once likened LA to 'a huge desert encampment', which captures exactly its improbable amalgam of the epic and the primitive.

I have been travelling here three times each year for fifteen years – approaching it first across the Atlantic from London, then across the Pacific from Sydney – and each descent towards the city continues to prompt a slight quickening of the pulse.

Los Angeles remains an elusive realm of paradoxes, a *noir* place in the sun. It has some of the most distinguished twentieth-century architecture in the world, which is routinely demolished to be replaced by ersatz retro buildings. It is dominated by Hispanic history, culture and language, yet few of the non-Latinos who still make up the majority of the population take any interest in it. (For many of those west of the Beverly Hills city boundary, this curiosity extends to little more than the dozen words they employ to communicate with their maids.) If it were to float away from the remainder of the United States it would be one of the richest countries in the world, but the poverty is palpable, the despair never more than a room away from a handgun.

In its unerring horizontality, it feels above all like a city of the future; a model for the way all cities will be in the next century. For much of the past one, it has axiomatically been the land of dreams, the place where people go to become somebody else. And while it is true that practically everyone here claims some remote connection with the movie business, it is always intriguing to discover the arcane nature of the link. On my first visit, the taxi driver on the ride in from the airport told me that he had been served his breakfast that morning by a waitress in the San Fernando Valley who claimed to have given James Mason a blow-job at the Beverly Wilshire Hotel in 1953. His account, delivered in the impartial monotone of someone no longer capable of being surprised, did not invite closer enquiry.

The white zone is for the immediate loading and unloading of passengers only. It follows that the first words one hears on a tape loop outside the international terminal are also the first lines of a motion picture – the great joke movie *Airplane!* – and it somehow sets the tone for the surrealism of what is to come. Although there is a snap in the air, we rent convertibles, immediately identifying ourselves as both outsiders and idiots.

Stephan, Grant and I are here because we are obliged to show the 'director's cut' of the film to Michael Kuhn, the president of PolyGram's film division, and to Russell

Schwartz, the president of Gramercy Pictures, the PolyGram-owned (with Universal) American distributor of many of PolyGram's movies. As we have transferred the film negative to tape to enable the picture to be edited by Sue Blainey on a rapid-access computerised system, and as we have been unable to afford to print up the corresponding film footage, we are screening what might be mistaken for a poorly pirated video, with primitive sound and enough visual blemishes to suggest that the duplicating engineer ate a pizza on it. This is not the ideal introduction to the widescreen enormity of our cross-dressing Outback epic.

We wait for Kuhn and Schwartz at the Adikoff Theatre in Beverly Hills, where there is a 'video imaging unit' which throws a larger image when projected on to a cinema screen. We play with colour, brightness, contrast, sound – anything that may enhance the limited effectiveness of what we have to show. It feels absurd to be 'rehearsing' a tape, but this is precisely what we are doing.

Stephan keeps us amused by telling us about his visit earlier in the day to the Disney studios, referred to by discontented writers a few years back as Mouschwitz. In obeisance to the corporate Christmas, the messengers on the lot were all wearing mouse ears, and Stephan walked into his pitch meeting in the main building through a frontage of seven columns, each being held up by one of the seven dwarfs. The discussion which followed could only be a disappointment. It was.

The arrival of Kuhn and Schwartz prompts the familiar hyperactive banter with which people in the movie business try to conceal their unease with each other, and it is a relief when the film is under way, if only for a minute or so.

It is a vulnerable stage in a picture's life, because although it is cut together in sequence it has no density. A film can only surprise and seduce when it is seen completed on the big screen. Right now, it looks and sounds quite dreadful. One is frequently being reassured by movie executives that they are accustomed to making the imaginative leap between a rough cut and a finished film. To believe this is to capitulate to a lifetime of disappointment. Here we are also up against an additional obstacle: the absence of any kind of scale. Even with the assistance of the 'video imaging unit', we are projecting *Florence of Arabia* on to an area not much larger than a lobby card, a problem we expect David Lean did not encounter when he showed his cut of *Lawrence* to Columbia over three decades earlier.

When the screening ends, the manner is cheerful but the body language is guarded, leaving us unsure of their reaction. Schwartz says that there are too many musical numbers, a disconcerting observation to make about a film musical with only four complete routines. He would cut the climactic Abba number. Kuhn tells us that he quite enjoyed the film, but that to assess it properly he will need to see it on a big screen, which I remind him that our post-production schedule will not give him an opportunity to do. Both say that they found the sequence in which the bus breaks down in the desert too long. As this has at its centre a montage which is the finest piece of pure moviemaking in the whole picture, I prepare to start arguing. Sensing the seeds of a confrontation, Stephan says it may feel that way because of the pacing of the scenes around it: he will look at it again closely, taking their comments into consideration. I am struck by the switch in our traditional roles: it is the director who ritually protests changes to his cut, and the producer who adopts the conciliatory stance. Stephan has clearly taken to heart, or at least to head, the lessons learnt from *Frauds*.

We walk around the corner for a drink at the Beverly Wilshire – once famed as the hotel where Warren Beatty kept a permanent suite, now better known as the capitalist fairytale castle in which Richard Gere holed up with Julia Roberts in *Pretty Woman* – before driving to a staff Christmas party at Michael Kuhn's house, up one of those serpentine streets behind the Beverly Hills Hotel. There is no other city on which it is considered so important to look *down*, not merely as part of the codification of wealth and power, but because the place really only makes sense when you can see it all. As we stand in the garden, the shimmering carpet of lights and the dozen planes one can see at any moment criss-crossing overhead against the night sky give Los Angeles an unsettling resemblance to its portrayal in *Blade Runner*.

Kuhn is an amiable host to his staff, and to us. He puts on an Abba album in winking acknowledgement of our presence, and he punctuates repeated references to his diet by visits to the food table and refills of Coca Cola. He shows us around the house, making jokes about its size as evidence that he is still above it all. His walk-around dressing closet is particularly striking – one could hold a small dance class in it – and he tells us it looked very odd when he had recently moved in and it contained only a couple of suits and a few shirts.

Leaving the party hungry, Stephan and I review the day

at the Columbia Bar and Grill near Paramount, whose instant table availability and correspondingly wide-open spaces bespeak a restaurant whose scene as a location in *The Player* was left on the cutting room floor. It closes a few months later.

There are two things on which one can always rely when arriving in London during the week before Christmas. One is that it will be raining. The other is that an IRA bomb scare, with which the city has been living with increasing familiarity for over two decades, will interrupt every journey made on public transport. (A third is that a ghastly record will be at the top of the charts in anticipation of Christmas week. This year it is the nauseating Mr Blobby, a large pink blow-up doll whose PR woman has officially become an item with Prince Edward, by doing so potentially sabotaging quite a good joke in the movie.)

Here our version of the film is to be shown to Stewart Till, the head of PolyGram's international division, and to the people at Manifesto – which is about to change its name to the prosaic PolyGram Film International – whose support helped to keep the project buoyant when it was a floating anomaly in the corporate system, unattached to any of PolyGram's wholly owned production companies.

There is no 'video imaging unit' in London, so we are screening the picture on three television monitors in a small preview theatre, which works with surprising effectiveness. The improved presentation and the increased audience numbers make us confident that the laughs will come more fluently, and that the movie will have a more perceptible overall impact.

This turns out to be the case, despite the absences of

Michael Kuhn – at a board meeting, after promising to see the film again with his other colleagues present – and Aline Perry, who runs Manifesto and is in Paris on a family matter. We say nothing, but we are not happy. After flying halfway across the world to show people a version of the film we would prefer to keep to ourselves, we expect them to be present when we arrive.

We have lunch with Stewart Till afterwards in a large restaurant full of florid-faced businessman next door to PolyGram's head office. Till admits that he was an early opponent of the film, so it is gratifying to hear him enthuse about it so unequivocally. Even when we plant a potential criticism in his head ('Do you not find all the swearing and abuse in the first half an hour a turn-off?'), he deflects it disarmingly ('No, I think it helps us like the characters more when they soften in the second half.')

Although there are no paper hats in evidence Christmas office parties are clearly raging around us, so we drink wine with lunch. This is not a good idea. We are peevish and testy at the subsequent meetings with PolyGram, a condition exacerbated by the British idea of central heating, which is to turn all office buildings into Turkish baths.

Michael Kuhn walks into a discussion we are having about soundtrack album business. Although he is clearly not in a good mood either, we press him for more comments on the film. 'We don't know where we are,' he says irritably, alluding, we assume, to the city and country in which the movie begins. 'Audiences need to know where they are. In *Schindler's List*, they tell you where you are all the time. This film should do that too.'

We add it to our list of comments and leave town.

We are back in Los Angeles, hoping to catch a plane that will land us in Sydney on Christmas Eve. Michael Kuhn and Aline Perry are seeing the picture in the late afternoon London time, and we are to have a conference call with them mid-morning LA time, in Russell Schwartz's office at Gramercy. They are late (more rain, more bombs, city at a standstill, we speculate correctly), and as we wait Schwartz tells us he feels the Charlene song at the beginning should be cut. When the call finally comes through, Kuhn first reiterates the remarks he made after the earlier screening: it is slow in the middle and he will be unable to pass judgement until he sees it on the big screen. He is perturbed by the fact that the 'letterboxing' necessary to show films shot in anamorphic widescreen on a television monitor in the right ratio has further reduced the size of the image.

Kuhn makes a couple of other points. One is that it is too long. At this stage, even with a modest running time of 109 minutes excluding end titles, nobody ever says a film is too short. (The shrunken attention spans of the MTV and video generations has engendered a horror of the leisurely moment, however dramatically charged. This is further aggravated by reports of young people in malls shouting 'Fast forward!' at the screen, as if stranded at home without the remote.) The other is that the flashback in which one of the characters is revealed to have had a child-molesting uncle is not at all funny, he feels, a view reinforced more emphatically by Aline Perry, who wants the scene eliminated completely. 'All that matters,' says Kuhn, 'is whether or not the film is funny. To find out, we need to test it.'

My response is that there is a kind of test screening

intended to help the director reach decisions about how to cut certain scenes, and another to shape the marketing of the finished picture in the most effective way. The former is not of interest to us: it is the film we are confident we want. The latter can be done after we deliver it.

In any case, it is not possible to test screen in the US until after the movie is completed in mid-April, by which time we will be preparing for May's Cannes Film Festival, where we decided a year earlier to return with the film, if there was one.

The conversation ends. Everybody wants to go home, wherever it is. As we walk towards the car, Stephan becomes aware of a pattern in Schwartz's proposed cutting of Charlene, Bernadette's walk and Abba. 'What he wants me to do,' he says, struck by his discovery, 'is to get rid of the beginning, the middle and the end of the film.' We make a final detour to the William Morris Agency, where Stephan signs the contract that has been in discussion since the last Cannes Film Festival. It is probably the first important agreement in showbusiness history to be executed lying on the floor of the agent's office, without either a lawyer or a bottle of champagne present.

We arrive back in Sydney on Christmas Eve, as intended. Three days later, we will be back in the cutting room. On Christmas Day, Bondi Beach is host to 30,000 people who have brought tables, chairs, fridges, sofas, miniature pine trees and a makeshift disco powered by a generator in a rented truck.

For a moment, we have forgotten about the film.

January 17. Three hours before we are scheduled to land in Los Angeles, as a brilliant ribbon of orange begins to settle along the horizon, the announcement comes through.

There has been an earthquake in the LA area, we are informed, its epicentre in the San Fernando Valley, its reading an unconfirmed 5.5 on the Richter scale. Sections of freeways have collapsed, the airport is closed, our flight may be diverted. Leaving behind the dying embers of the Sydney bushfires, we are flying towards another catastrophe.

When the lights are switched on in the cabin, there is a second announcement. The earthquake, which occurred at 4.31 a.m. local time, was more serious than earlier reports suggested. Its intensity was a formidable 6.6, (subsequently 'upgraded' to 6.7 and, in some reports, 6.8), making it the worst wake-up call Los Angeles has had this century. Stephan, whose appetite for disaster borders on the pathological, can barely contain his excitement, unequalled since he flew into town towards the end of the riots nineteen months earlier.

At the airport, which has reopened shortly before our arrival, there is the kind of menacing hush one associates with those films set in cities that have suffered a population wipe-out. A handful of immigration and customs people abstractedly go through their motions. We are out of the building in record time.

A second later, or so it seems, we are already driving towards the city. The traffic lights are all blinking red, and the paucity of other vehicles gives an exhilarating edge to running the gauntlet. The scale of the devastation only begins to reveal itself with the first sight of the Hollywood hills, which are nearly engulfed by the smoke which rises from fires in the valley and rolls across the sky towards us.

The Cut

Continuous reports on the earthquake have taken over all radio stations, including those which customarily broadcast only music. A story about a motorcycle cop who died when he tried to switch freeways during the quake and found that the one he was transferring to was not there anymore is heard so frequently that it begins to take on a comic dimension, its tragic one having been eroded by repetition. An apartment building has collapsed and the death toll is rising. The airwaves are monopolised by the voices of seismologists, who speculate on aftershock prospects, and psychiatrists, who discuss post-traumatic stress disorder.

When we reach the part of the road which goes under the Santa Monica freeway overpass, we find it cut off by the freeway itself, which has completely buckled at various points, leaving the supporting pillars mangled underneath. As we navigate a way around it, we see people dismantling the wreckage, others walking the streets in their dressing gowns, many sitting in armchairs on the manicured little lawns outside their houses.

At the apartment building where we are lodging with friends, there is a power cut, as there is in most areas of the city, so we carry our cases up seven floors in the dark, avoiding the rubble of the collapsed ceilings. In the apartment itself, where our hosts are still shaken, there is no structural damage but objects have fallen off shelves and a large wall mirror has collapsed to the floor.

Since we have worked over most of the holiday period to return here for a one day stopover to show a re-edited version of the film, we assume that our afternoon appointment with Michael Kuhn and Russell Schwartz will not be affected by anything as trifling as the aftermath of a natural disaster.

I call Michael Hamlyn, who is not so sure that this will be the case. There is no electricity at the Gramercy offices where the screening will be held, and both Kuhn and Schwartz are apparently vacillating about whether they want to leave their homes at such a vulnerable time on what is in any case a public holiday. There is something primitive about an earthquake that unsettles everyone, but a popular theory postulates that it especially affects those who are most accustomed to being in control of their circumstances.

By the time the meeting is finally called off, Stephan and I have lost interest in having it. We drive up Sunset Boulevard in search of a restaurant that will serve us lunch. The few places that have a functioning kitchen are doing unprecedented business. Ben Frank's, a round-the-clock diner where I have never waited for a table for more than thirty seconds, has a ninety-minute wait, so we appease our hunger with a visit to Book Soup, a store so intoxicating in its abundance that one loses all track of time. Then it happens.

There is a low rumble and everything begins to shake: bookcases, walls, windows, light fixtures; worst of all, the ground itself. For a moment I consider the ignominious possibility of dying under an enormous pile of overwritten film biographies that have crashed down from the shelves. As the other customers drop their books and run into the street, Stephan, browsing in the crime section, is struck by a flying hardback, which turns out to be the biography of a serial killer. The aftershock measures 5.5, which would be a significant earthquake in any place that has not already experienced a 6.6 earlier in the day.

While seismic unrest is a long-acknowledged part of life in Southern California, the unexpected severity of this one has dislocated everybody. There is a social historian on the radio saying that unlike urban riots, which are divisive, earthquakes are an act of God that consistently bring out the benevolence in people.

This is not in evidence at Ralph's supermarket where the management – disturbed both by the prospect of post-quake looting, and by the litigation which would almost certainly follow an injury caused by falling groceries – has decided to allow nobody into the store. Instead, assistants collect shopping lists at the entrances and return with loaded trolleys. Standing in a parking lot full of people waiting for their food to materialise, we decide that starvation is a preferable option. Fortunately, our dinner companions have decided otherwise.

The household – one of whom sleeps in a jogging suit and tennis shoes to save time if they need to abandon the building – awakes the following morning to a 4.7 tremor and to the data of the past twenty-four hours: 46 dead, damage estimated at $30 billion and – the 'upbeat' note – 73 arrests, compared with 534 on an average day.

Californians are a tirelessly explicit breed, for whom the world constantly needs to be assessed and quantified. What becomes clear from the tone of reporting is that, while the pioneering spirit that brings people to Los Angeles also makes them uniquely equipped to deal with disaster, part of the understanding is that the disaster should rapidly recede. The strength of the aftershocks reveals it is not to be the case.

Making Priscilla

The film business has come to a standstill. Warner, Disney and Universal, the three studios closest to the epicentre, have closed for the day.

Its favoured grazing holes, however, are open for lunch, including the Ivy, the restaurant whose location scene in *The Player* was *not* left on the cutting room floor. It is virtually impossible for a stranger to reserve a terrace table here, but today most of the restaurant's regular diners are too busy surveying damage or making insurance claims to show up, so there is no difficulty.

The screening at Gramercy has been rescheduled for this afternoon. We discuss our plans with Michael Hamlyn and decide that if Kuhn and Schwartz approve the cut of the film there is no need for me to travel to London, where Manifesto's endorsement of this approval will by then have become a formality. Since we are in a city where wisdom and banality become indistinguishable in their reductive mutation into slogans, I propose that this afternoon's be COLLUSION NOT COLLISION. Having bristled with pugnacity at the slightest criticism on our last visit, I have resolved to let people speak without interruption, to listen to what they say, to consider before responding, to accommodate their good ideas. Then to do whatever we believe is right.

We know that we have at least dealt with the question of overall length. The picture is running at just under a hundred minutes without end titles, nearly ten minutes shorter than the version we showed four weeks earlier.

When the first laugh resonates around the room a few minutes into the picture, I exhale silently, relieved that it will not require arm wrestling over pits of scorpions to convince them that this is the film. A friend of Kuhn's, who has otherwise enjoyed it, says it may have three minutes or so of 'air', which means he thinks it is still a little long. But there are no complaints about the pace of the middle section or about the musical numbers, and Schwartz chortles heartily at the now truncated, and funnier, child-molesting-uncle flashback, deflating Kuhn's remaining reservations. Schwartz also believes that we may have a hit film, and tells Stephan this as he accompanies him out to the parking lot.

Preparing to drive away, we realise that the curfew announced earlier in the day has already begun and that it will be impossible to find anywhere to eat. Kuhn, who recognises a pathetic sight when he sees one, invites us back to his house for pasta and red wine.

It is difficult to determine how much of the evening is a consequence of alleviated quake-anxiety, and how much is simply the right combination of five people fuelled by robust cabernets, but Kuhn is transformed for a couple of hours into the best imaginary chat-show guest in the world, leaving us laughing helplessly with accounts of what happened when his mother met Diana Ross in Las Vegas, what the take-off and landing procedures are for private jets at various airports around the world, and what people really think of a foul-mouthed comedian who makes enormous profits for PolyGram's video division.

By the time I am ready to drive out to the airport the following night, protracted exposure to earth tremors has begun to affect my gait, which now resembles that of a man who believes his feet are about to be swallowed by the ground. I meet a friend for a drink at what appears to be the only bar open in the deserted concrete and glass wastelands of Wilshire Boulevard.

I ask if life has begun to function again in the valley.

Many businesses have re-established trading that day, he says. Even the Universal tour has been running, except for one part: the earthquake ride is closed until further notice.

The Tests

Reluctant at this stage – after three months of fine cutting, music scoring, sound mixing and colour grading – to surrender the film to strangers in airline uniforms, with their boundless potential for sabotage, we carry the print on to the plane and place it in an overhead locker, inviting a certainly fatal cranial fracture if the containers were to tumble down during some sudden flight turbulence over Tahiti. (The sitar player Ravi Shankar used to circumvent this problem by buying a first class seat for his instrument, and keeping its belt fastened throughout the journey.)

There are few moments in the life of a movie when one is more *physically* protective of it than this. It is the final day before distributors and audiences begin, in their different ways, to subsume it; the eve of three crucial screenings which will together determine its future in the United States and, as a consequence, everywhere else.

The first, on the afternoon of our day of arrival, is a private show for friends in Los Angeles and for our still vacillating American distributor Gramercy, whose officially adopted neutrality towards *Priscilla* until the finished picture has been seen and approved is beginning to diminish the lustre of their privately declared enthusiasm. The second is a test screening, the results of which will be used to sanctify or vilify the movie, regardless of its fundamental qualities. The third is a presentation at the San Francisco Film Festival, where we are confident that on a Saturday night in a big, noisy, predominantly gay theatre the response will at least be demonstrative.

Still exhilarated by the tremendous reception the film received at its first screening in Sydney the previous week – to which we invited cast, crew and anybody we thought might be fun – we are reassured to see that LA is still standing. The Santa Monica freeway, between whose collapsed pillars we had attempted to pass our cars on the drive into town three months earlier, has recently reopened ahead of schedule and the city is buoyant with accomplishment. Haunted for a moment by the receding spectre of a 'video imaging unit', I realise it is caused by a return to the same screening room in Beverly Hills where we showed the director's cut on tape. If the film is not liked tonight, I conclude philosophically, I will continue to carry the cans. If it is, they will travel in their own limo.

Finally, there is sufficient money left in the budget to allow for paid accommodation. So, for the first time since we began travelling in connection with the film, Stephan and I can afford a hotel. I used to stay at Ma Maison, whose lively bar, pioneering voice-mail system and bewildering check-out gift of a baguette made it a singular experience. (One wondered what happened to the baguette when its recipient boarded a plane. Was it stored in the overhead compartment? Under the seat in front, where it might protrude mysteriously between the feet of the forward passenger? Or checked in, so that it turned up among the suitcases on the baggage carousel with a label around its crust?)

The Tests

A more seductive deal, however, is offered by the Nikko, about which, for reasons of complete recognition, I have word-perfect recall of Baz Luhrmann's endorsement in an Australian edition of *Vogue* he once edited: 'In the middle of a production, you're fear-ridden, really. So you want to be in a place where you feel supported.' It helps that everything in the place works perfectly, much of it from a bedside telephone into which most of the hotel services are programmed, allowing one to adjust the room temperature, for example, from a completely supine position.

The first person we meet in the hotel lobby is our French subtitler Henri Béhar, who picks up Stephan, twice his height, and twirls him around adoringly, to the embarrassed bewilderment of the Japanese businessmen waiting to check in. During the final days of last year's Cannes, Stephan came across Henri pressed up against a wall outside a restaurant tongue-kissing the chef, whose toque was bobbing around with pleasure. Henri came up for air, greeted Stephan and returned to his business.

While they amuse each other, I wander over to the concierge's desk, which is dominated by a large, decoratively presented basket of beers from around the world, a kind of United Nations of carbonated froth. 'Bet you wish you were getting that,' she quips mechanically, observing my curiosity. 'I wonder who the lucky bastard is,' I respond by rote. Later, in Stephan's room – where he stands at the window spellbound by the network of enormous pipes on the roof of the tiny Fatburger shack across the road – I find that *he* is the lucky bastard, except for one thing: he does not drink beer. His 'friends at William Morris', by whom the gift was sent, have not researched him well.

117

The Adikoff screening, comfortably full, is a success. People find the film both funny and touching, equally important factors if one is to have an American comedy hit. In the 90s, it appears that making people laugh is no longer sufficient, as evidenced by the ingratiating softheadedness of the final reels of even the better US comedies.

Like a spurned suitor unable to say goodbye, I take the print back to the hotel afterwards and hide it under the bed. The limo can wait.

A Sunday morning drive along nearly deserted streets up to Book Soup to collect the weekly edition of *Variety*, a pleasant ritual made more potent in this case by expectation. The colour transparency of the three drag queens with their backs to the camera at the top of Kings Canyon has been reproduced across half a page, and it looks terrific. It is the first major publicity for the film, and it is certain to create curiosity around the world in the thirteen days between now and the midnight screening in Cannes. Intoxicated with possibilities, I keep reopening the paper at the photograph.

We meet Michael Hamlyn at a restaurant in Venice which exhibits paintings by, among others, Joni Mitchell, the chronicler, in whatever medium, of a kind of freefloating LA reverie universes away from the gangs that stalk the adjacent streets. We agree on the issues which need to be resolved with Gramercy the following day, then walk around a neighbourhood in which territorial boundaries can be crossed in the length of a block.

What a strange city this is. The court case currently monopolising the press's attention is about which of two men – a garment company proprietor or an actor-turned-songwriter – invented phosphorescent underwear. There are, of course, plentiful punning opportunities, from lawyers 'filing unusual briefs' to judge and jury 'getting to the bottom of it all', with experts brought in to explain glow-in-the-dark crotchless panties and the lights turned out in the court so that these can be demonstrated.

The sense of dislocated absurdity is infectious: there is a parallel version of every moment. Later, driving along Beverly Boulevard at night near the New Beverly Cinema where *Reservoir Dogs* is often shown, Stephan sees a number of men in black suits walking along the road together. He thinks they are the kind of deranged fans that dress up like the characters in the movie, the way they do at *Rocky Horror Picture Show* screenings. They turn out to be Hassidic Jews on the way back from the synagogue.

There are a few questions we want to ask Gramercy, so we do. Where are the people who are attending the recruited screening recruited? (Shopping malls, mainly.) Why are there no 17 to 21-year-olds included in the otherwise demographically exhaustive preview audience? (Not our primary target group, it appears.) Why is nobody from the distribution company going to the San Francisco festival with us? (Two people volunteer to do so.) How are the ticket sales doing? (Quite well, but they would benefit from some promotion.) Is Gramercy releasing the film or not? (Everyone would like to, but first it must be tested. PolyGram corporate policy.)

It is a strange, rather fractured encounter, the kind shared by people who have much to accomplish together without yet knowing each other well. There is a great enthusiasm for the movie, but one feels that until the preview validates everyone's confidence this will remain a little muted. When we are shown a rough cut of the proposed trailer, Stephan and I fall out of our chairs with unison shouts of disbelief when we see it has revealed the fact that Tick has a son. The point of a trailer is surely to tantalise people into wanting to see the movie, not to give away everything that happens in it. While realising that the parallel is a little strained, I point out that what they have done would be rather like Miramax letting everybody know in the trailer of *The Crying Game* that Jaye Davidson has a dick, the picture's key marketing secret.

Quite rightly, Gramercy does not want to restrict the film's wider potential by making the initial marketing too comprehensively gay, so we discuss single images that convey the tone of the movie without, as the term goes, 'ghettoising' it: frill-necked lizards, echoing the outfits our trio wears during the third costume change of 'Finally'; the feather hitting the rock in the desert, which someone says looks sad. Until then, it has never occurred to me that a feather could look sad.

Discussing the best date on which to open the film, we agree that the original Gramercy preference of early October is out of the question because Johnny Depp in (and as) *Ed Wood* is scheduled for release on October 7, and it is clear that once Depp has been seen in a skirt and an angora sweater – the favoured outfit of the eponymous cross-dressing director Edward D. Wood Jr – our lot will not look so hot, or, more importantly, so surprising. September 2 is the opening date of *It's Pat – the Movie* starring the androgynous character from

Saturday Night Live. Paul Rosenfeld, the big man who runs Gramercy's theatrical distribution, vigorously denies that it represents any competition. '*Pat the Fucking Movie*,' he snarls, 'is going to be dead in a week.' Amidst the slippery evasiveness of film business speculation, we appreciate his from-the-hip manner, and he will turn out to be right.

When the office clears of everyone but Russell Schwartz, I decide to conclude some important unfinished business. I remind him that, as we are not receiving an advance from Gramercy, we are entitled to shop the film around and, if offered an advance of a million dollars or over, we can accept it. How does he feel about this? He surprises me a little with his speed and snap. 'I won't hear of it,' he says imperiously. Given the rewarding back-end terms we have in the existing deal, his determination suits us fine. For the moment.

While broadly in favour of test screenings for the vital clues they can give movie makers in resolving areas of uncertainty, I resent the way that they have incrementally helped to squeeze the distinctiveness out of motion pictures, and the manner in which studio executives have used them as a scientific stick with which to beat directors around their artistic heads.

Since *Star Wars* (1977) raised the threshold of aspiration on the financial return of a film, the use of research for everything from determining content to changing endings has created a pathological fear of deviating from the consensus, however often it may have been proved to be wrong. Although Hollywood has always used previews in some form – they were employed, famously, to justify the evisceration of Orson Welles' *The Magnificent Ambersons* – it is only in the past seventeen years that they have taken on some of the more unsettling qualities of organised religion.

Consider some of the extraordinarily diverse and individual studio movies made in the first half of the 70s, before *Star Wars* – Coppola's *The Godfather* (1 & 2), Rafelson's *Five Easy Pieces*, Bogdanovich's *The Last Picture Show*, De Palma's *Carrie*, Scorsese's *Taxi Driver*, Penn's *Night Moves*, Russell's *The Devils*, Mallick's *Badlands*, Nichols' *Carnal Knowledge*, Pakula's *Klute* or Altman's *Nashville* – and think how easily the evaluation cards of a single unsympathetic movie audience in San Diego or Long Beach could have led to their statistic-endorsed emasculation.

The first test screening of *I'll Do Anything*, James L. Brooks' ambitious musical comedy about the film business, was a disaster, with a reported seventy walk-outs. Brooks is an unswerving believer in the preview process, and has often said that he cannot cut a picture without it. Identifying the musical numbers as the problem, he removed most of them to see if the storyline and characters still came across. It helped a little, so his plan was to start reintroducing the songs over successive screenings to assess which ones worked. Six previews later, he had only one song left in the film, which turned out to be a box-office flop anyway. It may well also have failed had the musical numbers been retained, but the erosion of Brooks' confidence meant that it was worse than a flop: it was a compromised, truncated flop.

A memo we receive before leaving Sydney has already instructed us on how to drive to the Beverly Connection, where the preview is to take place. The company supervising the test is the National Research Group, and the appetiser-synopsis is lively with marketing bites: 'a new comedy adventure is kicking up its heels ... this road is not paved with asphalt but with sequins. Prepare yourself for a comedy that just may change the way the you think, the way you feel, and most of all, the way you dress.' Paraphrased, the last sentence plainly has possibilities as a trailer and poster copyline.

The driving instructions are wasted on us as the theatre is a five-minute walk from the hotel. A new photo of my baby daughter has arrived, which I put in my inside pocket – absurdly close to the heart – for good luck. The lobby is full of men in blazers with walkie-talkies, which prompts me to wonder if we have taken a wrong turning and ended up at an electronic surveillance convention. I look around to check if the demographic conforms to what we were told: 25 per cent aged 21–24, 25 per cent 25–29, 25 per cent 30–34, 25 per cent 35–49. It looks about right, although some are clearly younger than 21 or older than 49. There is sprinkling of fistfuckers with moustaches and leathers – including one with a stetson – and I relish the prospect of one day having the film play to an audience consisting entirely of drag queens: a movie showing to its mirror image, rather like seeing *Die Hard* with hundreds of men in grubby singlets with a weakness for climbing through the bowels of skyscrapers. Perhaps in San Francisco.

I read a questionnaire, a very general one as we are not using this preview for reasons other than to determine whether or not the film is liked and why. On some circulated sample forms I have seen, even with the titles and actors' names erased, the more specific questions tend to betray the identity of the film. The response card for *The Bodyguard*, for example, listed among the descriptions of the (blanked out) Kevin Costner character: 'reluctant to work with celebrities'.

We stand at the back of the theatre as the red velour curtains part, holding our breath so hard that it leaves a surfeit of oxygen for everybody else. Under a minute into the main titles, there is a glorious moment which prompts a relieved exhalation. When we cut wide to Hugo Weaving as Mitzi for the title card – revealing the full extent of his silvery curves in a dress which looks like a hand-me-down from the early Supremes – there are ripples of applause and amusement. Not long after, Bernadette's line 'a cock in a frock on a rock' – delivered with winningly weary disdain by Terence Stamp – brings the house down.

From then on, just about everything seems to work: the lipstick gag, the Broken Hill hotel room and pub scenes, the bus-top opera (applause), the Aboriginal campfire (roars of laughter and applause) and, to my delight, the Abba turd joke. The scene is timed perfectly by Terence and Guy Pearce, and the audibly dawning horror among the audience that the pay-off is going to be every bit as tasteless as they are dreading is one of the great repeat pleasures of subsequent viewings.

I wonder how an American audience will respond to the sight of a Filipino woman firing ping-pong balls out of her vagina to a riotously appreciative male bar crowd. I look at Stephan at the start of the scene and we exchange cartoon mannerisms of fear and dread, but it goes down well, except with a Filipino couple, who walk out. There are more big laughs: the shot of the Queen's portrait, the binoculars at the bus window, the cake out in the rain, Terence's little flourishes in the dressing room, and Hugo's fully extended frill-neck during 'Finally', which is punctuated by applause throughout.

After the end titles and final gag – for which, despite having alerted the projectionist, the house lights are already on – everything goes intimidatingly quiet. While the audience fill in their forms, I amuse myself by remembering the story recounted in Budd Schulberg's *What Makes Sammy Run?* about the three studio yes-men who are asked for their opinion after a preview. The first says it is without doubt the greatest picture ever made. The second says it is truly magnificent. The third is fired for saying he only thinks it is great.

A man in a leisure suit from National Research Group, who is monitoring the collection of the scorecards, finally gives us the nod: 'It doesn't get any better,' he purrs conspirationally. Dan Ireland, who has already selected the film for the Seattle Film Festival, considers Terence Stamp's performance outstanding, and notes his resemblance to Meryl Streep. Others will say he looks like Glenn Close. I call Terence later and inform him of his escalating glamour quotient.

By the time my attention is back in the theatre, a 'focus group' of twenty people and a moderator – one of those men who has done too many self-awareness courses – are discussing 'the characters' true sexuality'. One person thinks that the drag queens' climb at the end is a little anti-climactic; the rest disagree. Nineteen say that the movie is neither too fast nor too slow: it moves just right. One says that it moves a little slowly, but several people in the group begin to argue with him and he changes his mind. Most importantly, it appears to have given everyone pleasure. As one focus group member puts it, the film has 'a lot of feelings'.

Stephan, ready to gag at this point, is delighted when someone compares it with Hal Ashby's *Harold and Maude*, a movie which strokes the raw nerve of a childhood in which he frequently feigned his own death to attract his parents' attention.

Afterwards, I am handed the handwritten summary sheets: 45 per cent of the audience found the picture 'excellent' (against a NRG norm of 25), 34 per cent 'very good' (norm 30), giving us 79 per cent in the top two boxes (norm 55). If you add 'good' (14 per cent), we found acceptance with 93 per cent of the audience. Only three people disliked it, and three others walked out.

The next day, the film starts to travel by limo. Or so I like to think.

There is hardly any news in the movie business which travels as rapidly as that of a successful preview, and no individual quicker to respond to it than a hungry agent.

There is a question agents always ask as a prelude to stealing a client from other agencies: 'Are you happy?' I am called by someone to congratulate me on the results of the screening, and to inform me that she is part of a 'boutique' agency representing a 'small, select' group of writers and directors. She hopes that I will be interested in reading material written by her clients, and asks me to congratulate Stephan as well. 'Is he represented?' she asks. I tell her that he is, by Bobbi Thompson at William Morris. Then it comes: 'Is he happy?'

Bobbi has agreed to replace the beer with a bottle of

good champagne and a massage. The masseur has shown up in Stephan's room with an armoury of unguents and accessories. First he covers him in hot oils, then wraps him in plastic and blow-up leg-warmers so that he resembles a cross between the Michelin Man and a boiled ham. Then the phone rings. In the middle of his William Morris massage, it is ICM wondering if he is interested in talking.

At Gramercy, the test scores are confirmed to be very good indeed. Handing me the report, Russell Schwartz tells me that if one were to substitute the gay component of our audience with women, it is virtually the same result as for *Four Weddings and a Funeral*.

Accordingly, our Cannes planning meeting with them has a very different complexion from the spiky, tentative discussion of a couple of days earlier. The first item on the agenda is drag queens. We have already persuaded PolyGram in London to help bear the expense of getting three drag queens – Cindy Pastel, Strykermeyer and Portia – to Cannes for a documentary which is being made about them, and Gramercy now agree to pay them a fee of $100 for each of two performances they will give: one at the American Pavilion on the night of the screening, the other at the PolyGram villa after the distributors' dinner the following night. 'And they'll never have to pay for drinks,' adds the publicist Claudia Gray. Stephan widens his eyes in simulated horror. *'Don't* tell them that,' he says like the appalled parent of delinquent children. 'If you do, they'll drink so much they'll get completely trashed and start licking Stewart Till's face in front of the distributors.' This is a prospect we all relish, so drinks will be on the house.

As we arrive at the film's first LA press screening, arranged for that evening, each reel of Robert Redford's *Quiz Show* is being carried out by security guards as it finishes, a rigorous policing of potential bootlegging that is clearly not being applied to our picture. *Quiz Show* overruns, and there is a perceptible weariness in the waiting journalists by the time *Priscilla* starts fifteen minutes late. The response feels correspondingly muted by comparison with the two local screenings so far, and we are sitting behind an immobile man with a hairdo like Jack Nance's in *Eraserhead*, the back of whose head gives nothing away.

Depressed, I have dinner with the screenwriter Robert Mundy, who has better reason to be depressed than I do. *Twenty-One*, his ten-year-old screenplay based on the same incident as *Quiz Show*, is an outstanding script that will now probably never be made. I tell him that earlier in the evening I saw the cans of Robert Redford's film, but that security guards prevented me from getting any further. Mundy is part of a rare Hollywood species, an educated man who is not bitter, and he retains his flair for the epigram. When I ask him about Helena's, a private club in Silverlake popular with the fast crowd in the late 80s, he puffs ruminatively on his cigar and says, 'It was a place where people went to watch their agents dance.'

While neither of us have yet seen his agent dance, Stephan and I are seeing studio executives do so around their offices. Many of them, in accordance with Candice Bergen's memorable typecasting ('those tiny, intense executives'), are quite short.

Although the rituals of business courtship are fascinating, I can see no point in having conversations with people who are unable to make decisions. Crossing the parking lot towards the opulently redecorated Thalberg building on the Sony lot, we see a giant hoarding of Peter O'Toole as Lawrence, prompting thoughts about what he might have looked like in drag in the Outback. Then we really could have called it *Florence of Arabia*.

The posters which executives have on their walls, chosen from the studio's library of one-sheets, are usually a revealing barometer of both their self-image and their function within the studio. The person we see at Columbia has three – *Boyz N the Hood, Poetic Justice* and *El Mariachi* – and together they say 'in charge of minority filmmakers'. Stephan – a white boy from Sydney's North Shore with an appetite for big, expensive trash – could not be further away from this approach.

He has some fun at Amblin, where, instead of being cross-examined about *Priscilla* and *To Wong Foo*, he meets an executive who recently travelled to the Gay and Lesbian Mardi Gras in Sydney, and has just attended a fancy dress party to which he and his partner showed up as Holly Hunter and Anna Paquin in *The Piano*.

The most memorable encounter of all is not with a studio executive but with a studio security guard. Charcoal black in a smart navy blue uniform and a badge which identifies her as Alfreda Myers, she hovers behind both sides of a pillar at the entrance to the reception area of MGM/UA, the whites of her spying eyes appearing around it. She is the hidden camera, the silent watcher who misses nothing, and she turns up in parts of the building which Stephan feels sure can only be explained by the fact that she has her own secret corridors, enabling her to confuse people she is following by arriving before them at their destination.

We are both frightened and fascinated by her, and feel that on a subsequent visit we may fall in love completely.

We pick up Grant at the airport and drive up the coast road to San Francisco in a convertible. There are some weird sights along the way – a model trying to sell clothes to lunch tables of 'ladies' in Santa Barbara; a surfer on a contaminated beach near Guadalupe; Hearst Castle lighting up through low rain clouds at twilight; jets of spray coming through a rock in the rain at Big Sur; a coffee shop full of *very* strange people in Santa Cruz.

Arriving in San Francisco singing selections from *Can't Stop the Music* in the muted evening light, we hear that when the Gramercy people were pink-leafletting Castro Street near the theatre where the film will be shown, they offered one to a distinguished-looking man emerging from one of the many gay bars in the area. 'Of course I want to see it,' he barked, 'I'm one of the investors.'

There is a reception for everyone connected with the festival at Emporio Armani, and the sense of irregularity which will take over for the rest of the night is already in motion: we are standing around talking, eating and drinking among hundreds of thousands of dollars of Armani clothes, as models glide around us randomly.

Reeling from the excessive oxygenation of a day in the back seat of the convertible, compounded by the cold wine consumed among the clothes horses, we arrive at a dark, fast-lane restaurant called Bix. A young actress who lives close to her senses first tries to get up Stephan's nose as much as possible, then switches her attention more literally to his ear, into which she plunges her tongue while still chewing her food. The evening deteriorates with increasing hilarity from then on, turning ugly only when the actress attempts to rape Stephan on a pool table in a late-night bar.

The Castro Theatre audience are more prepared for the film than we could ever have imagined, yet not so prepared that they fail to be surprised. It is a dream screening. The crowd is so exuberantly responsive to the movie that it begins to resemble an interactive show rather than a motion picture, and at the end Stephan is practically carried from the theatre on the shoulders of his adoring public. It is a night for punching the air.

David Stratton's review in weekly *Variety*, which on a Sunday is available only in Los Angeles, has been faxed up at our request. For a moment, it seems slightly muted, less than the all-cylinders rave I was hoping for, but I send a copy up to Stephan's room and he is delighted with it. It is pretty good. Stratton calls it 'a cheerfully vulgar and bitchy, but essentially warmhearted road movie with a difference . . . a lot of fun', and he acknowledges several individual contributions.

The next morning I am awoken by a call from Russell Schwartz. *Daily Variety* has reprinted the previous day's piece from the weekly edition and the *Hollywood Reporter* review – written, we are astonished to find, by the man whose post-modernist beehive we sat behind at the press screening – is also a rave. He calls the film 'drenchingly delirious, wickedly pithy, a splendid amusement', noting also its poignant elements. Schwartz reads me the draft of a media release announcing that the picture will be distributed in the US by Gramercy and asks me for a quote. I have no interest in the corporate logorrhoea that appears between quotation marks in trade press announcements. 'Just write what you like,' I say.

By now breathing rarified air, we fly to Cannes.

Cannes: The Return

Priscilla

This time there is a car waiting. Indeed, there are two cars waiting, as well as several photographers and a small television crew, which gathers spectators as it shuffles and swerves through Nice airport. We are hitting the ground running, with a follow camera.

Waiting for the plane in London, I remark to Stephan that, while we will return to Cannes with bigger, perhaps better pictures in the future, we will never again be assured as open a licence to boundless fun with a film as we have with *Priscilla*. After a disagreement with PolyGram about which section and time-slot within the festival would most benefit the movie – one night I spend an hour arguing with them from the lobby phone of a Sydney hotel, while my dinner companions consume an entire meal in my absence – we have ended up where we wanted in the festival. First Saturday at midnight, official selection, out of competition: all of the amusement, none of the pressure.

In Cannes, every palm tree and lamppost along the seafront promenade, the Croisette, has already been wrapped with a *Priscilla* DRAG IS THE DRUG poster. It has been a commando operation of unparalleled thoroughness, accomplished with kinetic speed by shadowy figures in the night, and it is evident even at this early stage how much curiosity it is prompting about the film.

133

As I did on arrival last year, I have lunch with Hercules Bellville, who understands better than anyone how, despite the influx of neophyte hustlers each year, Cannes fundamentally revolves around tradition, ritual and a kind of ironic familiarity in which one is both above the nonsense and in it, equal parts observer and participant. Landmark absurdist figures like the inseparable mother and daughter in leopardskin, widely understood to operate as a courtesan double act, have by now acquired a picturesque dignity, prompting the rumour that they have been given festival passes this year. At the next festival perhaps they will be appointed presidents of the jury.

During a meeting with PolyGram, I am perturbed to see the word 'Classics' on our new sales agent's business card. Except when used as a marketing euphemism for 'old', 'classic' is a suffix most commonly employed by studios with arthouse divisions, reflecting correspondingly diminished box-office expectations. We see our movie as a popular entertainment and do not wish to have it perceived as 'specialised' in any way. We are reassured that it will be sold as a commercial picture, and the high initial offers appear to corroborate this.

In the congestion and effort of completing the film in time for the screenings in the US and Cannes, some delivery materials, mainly routine documents, have not yet been supplied, and the film's lawyer Martin Cooper and I work our way through these with PolyGram's post-production supervisor. My attention strays towards the torpid hum of another meeting being held across the terrace, while under a parasol at a table on the grass a perspiring distributor is attempting without success to reduce the asking price of a film for which he is bidding.

Occasionally, we are interrupted by requests for the supervisor's presence in another part of the building. 'Steve, come upstairs quickly,' says a frantic sales executive, 'we're having a lot of trouble with the Turks.' With all the potential for pleasure in the build-up to Saturday's midnight screening, I begin to begrudge the way in which procedural drudgery is eroding the energy.

The gathering storm clouds are dissipated briefly by an encounter in a hotel lobby with Nik Powell, the executive producer of *The Crying Game* and a longtime friend. Discussing, inevitably, the transvestite parallels in our respective films, he tells me that when he was first seeking American distribution, the then president of Paramount rejected *The Crying Game* without ever being aware of the movie's crucial twist: that the leading lady is also a leading man. The studio chief left the screening room, where he was watching the film alone, to take a telephone call seconds before the key scene and returned after it was over. As the moment is not referred to again, and the consequent change in the characters' behaviour is subtly developed, he had no idea that he had missed a moment that would soon make, in its way, film marketing history.

There appear to be even more DRAG IS THE DRUG posters around the town today, and it has not escaped the notice of a reporter from the *Los Angeles Times*, who corrects the claim: 'Any Cannes regular knows that positive buzz is the drug here, both for driving sales to film distributors and building audience awareness.'

Invigorated for a moment with positive buzz, I arrange a discussion in which Gramercy and our newly acquired Australian distributor Roadshow can work out how best to make their plans overlap to mutual benefit. Russell Schwartz has decided to open the picture in the US on August 10, a Wednesday rather than the more customary Friday, to give the film a chance to build up favourable word of mouth before the weekend. He gives me a preliminary marketing plan which reveals the intention of selling the film initially 'to the gay and art film audience, followed by a push to cross the film over to the mainstream upscale audience.' The picture will be released in a series of expanding waves around the country, reaching its peak by the end of September. In addition to press, radio and television – initially only cable – advertising, there are to be life-size cut-outs of the three principals, nationwide lip-synch/drag competitions and numerous merchandising items such as key chains in the form of high-heeled shoes. Depending on the scale of the release, the stages of the campaign completed and the corresponding money spent, Gramercy are estimating a North American box-office gross of anywhere between five and twenty million dollars.

Alan Finney of Roadshow, the distribution counterpart of a fire-and-brimstone preacher, has a view of the film which is simultaneously limitless in its enthusiasm and circumspect in its promotional boundaries. 'One of the most exciting, adventurous and satisfying movies to come along in years,' he affirms. 'It blends the musical, drama, comedy and "self-discovery" genres into one totally entertaining and thought-provoking entertainment experience, a statement and celebration of individual choice and the search for fulfilment.' His main concerns in reaching the widest possible audience are the dangers of hard sell and of positioning the picture as a movie about drag queens in as enduringly homophobic a society as

Australia. 'Contemporary, socially relevant, intelligent but not elitist, entertaining without compromising its content, challenging but not didactic, aware of its audience but not pandering to its expectations,' he concludes with a flourish. His emphasis is on frequent previewing in full theatres and building on the enthusiasm for the movie he feels sure will follow. He outlines the release date options through to the end of the year, listing the respective assets and liabilities. We agree generally that July is too soon to have a campaign ready, that August does not allow the possible critical acclaim and commercial success to percolate through from the US, and that November and December are too late to benefit from any momentum created by its screenings at Cannes. I favour early September, in the lead-up to the Australian school holidays.

There is a US press lunch for *Priscilla* at the American Pavilion, which I am interested in visiting principally because it has an 'interactive video kiosk' called Inter-Elvis in which one can 'interact' on touch screens with Elvis to access all kinds of information about the festival. Instead, I am steered around various tables to interact with the press, among whom there is a consensus that the few studios present are here mainly to meet with European money sources about sharing finance and splitting rights. This is an unusual reversal, as the overtures routinely flow in the other direction. It reveals that film budgets are now so far out of control that this may become the only way that studios will be able to afford to make their now preposterously expensive movies.

Mostly though, Cannes is being propelled by the usual delusions and lies, with *Variety* lamenting that the place is 'overrun by lawyers and agents, all so preoccupied with trying to screw each other on deals that they have no time for the kind of sexual scandals that once made Cannes so worthwhile.'

But there is one element which has never changed, one that, in many respects, characterises the festival better than any deal or sexual scandal: the photocall. This is, after all, the only place in the world where the former Mrs Stallone, Brigitte Nielsen, can still be guaranteed to attract a swarm of paparazzi wherever she goes. Approaching the Majestic Beach, we can see that our three drag queens – Cindy, Stryker and Portia – have already stopped the pedestrian traffic on the Croisette, and are being navigated with some difficulty through the onlookers. As Terence Stamp and I push our way down the steps towards the beach, a man recognises him.

Many people recognise Terence. An enduring presence among actors, his work in European films and his history with Cannes (*The Collector*, for which he won the Best Actor award in 1965, and *The Hit*, a Directors' Fortnight success in 1984) have made him a popular figure here, and he has not besmirched his lustre by attending the festival too often. But this man *particularly* recognises him. 'You remember me,' he says, unmistakably Italian, the three words a declaration rather than a question. 'Party scene. Fellini. *Toby Dammit*. You. Me.' Terence is gracious but keen to move on. Only in Cannes could an actor be stranded in a crowd with a bit-part player with whom he shared a screen moment twenty-seven years earlier. (It was only after Fellini's *La Dolce Vita* had conclusively established him at Cannes in 1960 that his films became populated by the grotesques for which his surname doubled as an adjective, leading some to conclude that he may have considered himself more a documentarian than a caricaturist.)

By the time Terence has joined Stephan, Hugo Weaving and the drag queens on the pier, a near riot has developed, with so many photographers and television cameramen shooting (and shouting) from so many angles that at one stage the wooden pier begins to buckle and someone falls into the water. A colour picture capturing this madness, by an adjacently positioned British photographer who realises his subject is not drag queens but other photographers, appears on the front page of the British newspaper the *Independent* the following morning.

Later we have dinner with Russell Schwartz and various Gramercy people at a restaurant called Le Moulin à Poivre, whose chef (*cuisine signée Gérard Guth*), in consonance with this most *auteur*ist of towns, dispenses a business card with his photo, in which he is wearing an impressive toque.

As if to demonstrate the connection between all things, Henri Béhar, no stranger to toques, shows up at our print rehearsal at the Salle Debussy later that night. It is clear he has done a splendid job in creating the French subtitles, and for each merely eccentric change ('raccoon' has mysteriously become 'panda'), there is a cleverly idiomatic one ('bats for both teams' is translated as 'double agent', as there are no French sports played with bats). The Salle Debussy, smaller than the main cinema, has the best screen-size-to-seats ratio I have ever seen, and the design of the theatre favours width, which in turn gives us an ideal Scope image.

In my exhaustion, I remember somebody telling me that

the director Emir Kusturica has a 'nap clause' in his contract, which officially permits him to take a snooze at certain times. I invent my own nap clause and invoke it immediately.

It is the morning before the big night. I am still having considerably less fun than I could be.

A trade magazine calls *Priscilla* 'the hottest ticket of the festival'. Soon, no doubt, it will be usurped by an even hotter ticket such as Quentin Tarantino's *Pulp Fiction*, which has shrewdly been programmed for the following weekend to keep the Cannes aristocracy, none of whom have seen it, from leaving early. I also note that there is a screening of what I assume is the Italian picture which Rupert Everett chose to do instead of ours, but it may be another one. It is called *Dellamorte Dellamore*, and in it Everett plays a reclusive cemetery caretaker who has to contend with the resurfacing of freshly buried bodies. There is a photograph of him naked holding a similarly naked (but dead) woman as if she were a musical instrument, prompting memories of Alain Delon's hilarious post-coital compliment to Marianne Faithfull in *Girl on a Motorcycle*: 'Your body is like a violin in a velvet case.'

The only striking thing about all the finished, half-made and completely imaginary films which are advertised at Cannes, is how many of them resemble each other. Two movies that day are represented by images of people having sex in water: traditionally but enthusiastically, in a shower (*Intruso*) and, more imaginatively, in a subterranean waterhole illuminated by candles (*Dark Tide*). A leaflet I am given also involves the promise of aquatic sex. Titled *Sailing Adventure*, 'the hottest

California girls' (unaccountably, a trademarked name, as if such a sequence of words could be owned) who are represented are seen either loafing around the decks in prodigiously inappropriate sailing outfits, or pulling at ropes in lacy underwear and full make-up.

With a pre-screening dinner at the PolyGram villa, a gathering at the American Pavilion during which the drag queens will perform, the movie itself, a drinks party following at two-thirty in the morning, and tomorrow's screening and dinner for distributors, the whole operation requires an exactness of orchestration that defies the customary chaos of Cannes life. Names are added, subtracted and transferred on dozens of lists before we are satisfied that the right people are attending each function. Afterwards, I discuss the renegotiation of the PolyGram licence agreement with Catriona Hughes of the FFC. We are in a coffee shop, perched on unstable canvas chairs inscribed with the misspelt names of Hollywood actors. I am sitting on Jacques Nicholson, she on Warren Batty.

At twilight we are taken by bus to the villa, the first stage in keeping our group together for the night, like a football team before an important fixture, or the members of a jury in an unusually sensitive trial.

After dinner we drive down to the American Pavilion, where far too many people have already assembled for what will be a chronically under-rehearsed show on a makeshift stage with rudimentary lighting. As we await the arrival of the drag queens, who are being escorted to the venue by Grant – relieved, no doubt, not to have been asked to perform again this year – we drink tepid white wine out of plastic beakers and smile tentatively at each other in the melée. Finally the trio are outlined behind the gossamer curtains, and, in a climate of complete chaos, begin the performance, in which each of them mimes to a song. Stryker – in a black and white dress embroidered with eyes – does a riveting burlesque variation on 'Me and Mrs Jones' and makes me blush a little by electing me as his front-row stooge, addressing the entire song at my forehead. Its fragmented, hit-and-miss nature would hardly qualify as a show at all in some circles, but this is precisely what distinguishes drag from more orthodox performance arts.

Television crews are wandering around talking to anyone slightly resembling, or related to, a celebrity. A British television presenter, Richard Jobson, whom I used to know when he was a young trainee rock star with Peter O'Toole affectations, interviews me. 'Ladies and gentlemen,' he deadpans to camera, 'this man taught me everything I know about drugs and alcohol.'

Someone gathers us together, and we make our way around the rear of the Palais, our arrival at the bottom of the steps which lead to the Salle Debussy being timed to coincide with the opening of the doors. When we reach the steps – drag queens in tow, the lights bouncing off their sequins on to Terence's immaculate white dinner jacket – the doors are still closed, and we are left standing in the street with hundreds of people just *staring* at us, instead of catching the fleeting, waving glimpse that they do with real celebrities.

We shuffle uneasily, telling jokes and looking back at a crowd now spellbound by the drag queens. Then it happens. Everybody who has been kept waiting begins a simultaneous rush on the staircase. Suddenly we are a mob, bouncing around like random atoms as we attempt to find a path through the bodies to the Palais door. Her temperament well equipped to deal with riots, Catriona Hughes takes my hand and pulls me through.

Although there is some laughter and applause during the screening, we are by now sufficiently spoiled by the response to the film in Los Angeles and San Francisco to find the audience a little muted. At the end, however, it reveals itself to be quite a different story. The ovation is so long, so resonant and so plainly *felt* that I look over to see Stephan getting a little teary. Everybody is on their feet applauding, and scanning the crowd for familiar faces I see Alan Finney recording it all with his video camera. Forgetting that reporters check their watches during standing ovations, modesty prevails over self-indulgence and we leave the theatre after a few minutes.

At a party across the road at the Majestic Hotel we hear that well over a thousand people are officially estimated to have been locked out of the Palais earlier. Charged by the success of the film, PolyGram executives glide around the room making introductions. While I would appreciate an unprompted acknowledgement from one of them that my decision to support an official selection midnight screening was the right one, instead I find myself shaking hands with Ted Field, one of the principals of Interscope, which produced *Three Men and a Baby* and epitomises a certain kind of confident middle-of-the-road Hollywood sensibility. He tells me he feels the picture could play anywhere in the United States. The challenge will be to get reluctant rednecks into the theatres in the first place. If we can do that, he says, word of mouth will take care of the rest. Across the room, Rupert Everett is being genuinely, awkwardly gracious about how much he enjoyed the movie he declined to be in a year earlier, and he particularly praises all the performances.

It has been an extraordinary night, and a long one. By the time it is over, nausea is setting in.

The distributors' gala screening the following day – the word 'gala' has a forebodingly starchy overtone – is the toughest so far. Stephan disappears during it, but some force field mysteriously prevents me from leaving the cinema. Although it will eventually become a form of addiction, I am still fascinated to see which jokes work with what audiences. By now, it is evident that if people laugh during the main titles sequence, the film will always take off from there, and the more noise is made during Guy Pearce's first appearance (his mincing desert-holiday limerick over the tune of 'Tararaboomdeay') the more hardcore-gay the crowd is likely to be.

At the decorous dinner which follows a number of distributors tell me how much they enjoyed the movie. Afterwards, the drag show held on the same lawn where Grant once entertained us is more elaborately staged than the performance at the American Pavilion and has much greater impact. Stryker performs a Laurie Anderson song in a leather *bustier* and dramatically tears off his blood orange wig to reveal shaved temples, while Cindy skips around the grass uneasily and Portia flirts with the PolyGram executives standing near the food table. When one of them begins pelvic-thrusting at her, I take it as a signal that the night is going to deteriorate.

Back at the hotel, stories from Monday's Australian papers have already been faxed through. PRISCILLA DRAGS CANNES TO ITS FEET is the headline in the *Sydney Morning*

Herald, whose report clocks in the standing ovation at three minutes while the other newspapers claim five, as if rival timings had been commissioned. The overall tone is highly enthusiastic, and I remember Alan Finney's perfect aphorism that while Australians may be notoriously ill-disposed to 'tall poppies', they love *growing* poppies. My favourite is a syndicated piece which ends by saying that 'director Stephan Elliott was not immediately available for comment as he was swallowed up in the late-night Croisette crowd.'

To develop a sense of proportion about all this – the film, after all, has only played to one preview and three festival audiences – I have breakfast with Alex Proyas, whose success is a little easier to quantify. His picture *The Crow* has just opened in America and has taken nearly twelve million dollars in its first weekend. The film's producer Ed Pressman, who does not drive, is being chauffeured around theatres in Los Angeles so that he can survey the lines outside.

Alex's short film *Welcome to Crateland* is in competition here, making it the first time Cannes has hosted a director in this section who at the same moment is breaking US box office records. The asset of all this is that there is already a message at the desk for him from the soon-to-walk mouseketeer Jeffrey Katzenberg. (The message reads: 'Chairman of Walt Disney Studios', as if that in itself were a message.) The liability is that he is being offered projects with titles like *Baseball Frankenstein*. Alex and I once tried to set up a movie together, with an even more ghastly title. It was called *Dial M for Monster*, a pastiche of those cheap 50s' science fiction pictures which had *noir* lighting only because they could not afford much *lumière*.

The dialogue was particularly unsavoury: a foul-mouthed alien says things like 'Suck the snotty end of my fuckstick' and 'Kiss my dead dog's ruby red asshole', which makes the grubby abuse of *Priscilla* seem anodyne by comparison.

Alex has a real hit movie. Although our film has been sold everywhere apart from places where they cut off the hands of cross-dressers, for the time being it is no more than a festival favourite, but at least we get to eat with interesting people. The director Alan Rudolph is here with his picture *Mrs Parker and the Vicious Circle*, financed by two rival companies, which he describes as 'like forced sex'. Rudolph is a rare creature in the contemporary film business because he speaks in complete sentences, a quality as archaic these days as cabin trunks and long courtships. He entertains us with stories about an executive so pathologically unable to do his own reading that he insisted on seeing 'coverage' of a three-page treatment.

I am halfway through a mouthful of sole when the building shakes, and for a moment Stephan and I feel that we are back in the Los Angeles earthquake. A glass awning above the main door has collapsed after being hit by a padlock and chain that has fallen from the roof of the building.

Later, we meet John Waters who, with the sleeping caterpillar which masquerades as a moustache over his top lip, radiates mischief as he tells Liberace stories. I tell him my own favourite: that by his last few years Liberace's innumerable face lifts caused the skin around his eyes to become so taut that he was unable to close his eyes to sleep. Waters cannot eclipse it.

In the evening, the drag queens are being filmed in various settings for the documentary, so I escort Portia from the Martinez Hotel to a nearby beach. In her pink swimsuit and Medusa wig, walking on heels so tall that she totters, she leans on my shoulder as we wander along together through the crowd, a middle-aged man in a tweed jacket holding up a giant drag queen: we are quite a sight.

Their first interview is on a pier with Ruby Wax, who is particularly fascinated by Cindy's son Adam. 'I have two pieces of advice for you,' she brays at the poor child. 'First, get yourself an agent. Second, get yourself a therapist.' Ruby asks Portia what she does when she is not being a drag queen. Portia laughs uproariously. 'Oh, you mean like in *Flashdance*: am I a welder by day?'

At a restaurant table in the old port, Terence and Hugo are interviewing Cindy and Stryker for the documentary cameras. Terence has just heard of the death of his friend the adventurer-businessman Frederik van Pallandt, whom he refers to as The Baron. In the late 50s and early 60s, Frederik had several sweet, folky chart hits in Britain with his then wife, Nina. Terence has known him since the 70s when they both lived in Ibiza, by which time both had retreated from the activities that had made them famous. In the receding light, Terence stares into the middle distance remembering his friend, speaking of him with affection and amusement without for a moment lapsing into the lachrymose. Frederik and his wife were shot on the day following his sixtieth birthday in what was later described as a professional killing.

Returning to the hotel hoarse with encroaching laryngitis, I find that there have been calls from Australian radio stations. Hotel phone rates militate against allowing oneself to be put on hold, so when they know I am in my room the stations ring again. As I wait for my part of the broadcast, I hear several moments of 'real' news. It all seems unsettlingly very far away.

Although our film is well known to be a comedy-musical about three drag queens crossing the Australian Outback, there is a photo in a trade magazine of a woman resembling the young Faye Dunaway earnestly holding one gun and pointing another; it is not clear at whom or what. The picture is captioned *The Adventures of Priscilla, Queen of the Desert*: perhaps it is the movie we should have made.

Stephan has been unsettled by an incident following a party at which his glib, hyperactive frivolity has got the better of him. Someone began to introduce him to an Australian film director he already knew well, and Stephan cut it short: 'Of course I know him,' he snapped, 'I used to bonk his wife.' This fatally careless remark – its absence of truth subordinated to its potential amusement value – has opened a Pandora's box of secrecy and suspicion, culminating in Stephan on his hands and knees the following morning on the Croisette begging the forgiveness of both director and wife.

This cartoon humiliation behind him, he meets me for dinner with an executive from Fox, to whom he proposes the idea of adapting Bret Easton Ellis's graphically grisly novel *American Psycho* as a musical. (This has become something of a habit with Stephan. When he is unable to think of an original angle or wants to sabotage a prospective work assignment, he invariably suggests

148

turning whatever it is into a musical.) While he goes to see *Muriel's Wedding*, I attend a party for the film *Sex, Lies and Democracy*. Images from the movie – involving various conjunctions of sex and history – are being projected on to a screen behind the dance floor while records are played by the club D J, an exercise which succeeds in deflating the sex, trivialising the history and neutralising the songs' own power of suggestion. The absolute nadir comes when Ray Charles' 'Hit the Road Jack' is heard over footage of Jews boarding concentration camp-bound trains.

The next morning's *Variety* comes out in favour of *Priscilla* over *Muriel's Wedding* in its assessment of the latter: 'With more than a little common ground artistically, musically and in origin (Australia), the film is vulgar to ill effect, while the drag comedy *The Adventures of Priscilla, Queen of the Desert* cheerfully uses its inherent vulgarity to hilarious ends.' This is the first critical comparison made between the films and it will not be the last, presaging a rivalry which will escalate from that moment on.

In acknowledgment of Terence's links with Italy – apart from his well-known work with Fellini and Pasolini, he also made pictures there with Dino Risi, Giuseppe Petroni Griffi, Armenia Balducci and others – our recently contracted Italian distributor has decided to hold a press conference. When I arrive, I realise that I recognise the distributor. By the time I have walked across the room to be introduced, I remember why. His name is Andrea Occipinti, and he plays the bullfighter who gives Bo Derek her first orgasm in *Bolero* and who, after being gored in the *cojones*, is restored with Bo's succour to full tumescence. He immediately feels like the right distributor for our movie.

Stephan arrives at the end of a dinner I am having with Alex Proyas and various colleagues and companions. Alex is on to the evening's umpteenth expression of contempt for the vapid hysteria and compulsive insincerity of festival life, whereas Stephan, just off the Cinergi yacht where Bruce Willis has been giving him the unsolicited benefit of his advice, is having the time of his life. It is an odd moment: two thirty-year-old Australian directors reacting in totally polarised ways to having money and attention thrown at them.

As we walk along the street afterwards, Stephan expresses his thanks for the first time since we began to work together eighteen months earlier. He tells me that he could not have done it without me, that I made an immense contribution both to the quality of the film and to the restoration of his self-confidence, and that he considers us a working team from now on. It is gratifying to hear, even if the moment (late, exhilarated, full of wine) does not encourage confidence in its gravity. When he disappears into a bar near the old port, I feel sure at least that he will have an interesting story in the morning.

He does, or at least he would if he were capable of connected speech. Piecing together a mosaic out of the madness, from changing declensions and unfinished clauses, it appears that the night involved numerous people, a scary car ride at some speed and a long walk back to town after escaping across a golf course at dawn.

Recovering in time to attend the William Morris cocktail party – where his agent Bobbi Thompson, who wooed him so effectively a year earlier, finally has the opportunity to steer him around rooms almost distended by the concentration of wealth and prestige – he stays on to accompany her to *Pulp Fiction*, directed by fellow Morris client Quentin Tarantino.

Afterwards, at a beach party in the middle of the night, like a regular at Helena's in the 80s, he finally gets to watch his agent dance, and having done so, joins her on the floor.

The Interlude

On the final day of Cannes – when the only people left are the disconsolate buyers and sellers who have failed to meet their targets, or expectant prize-winners and their retinues – we hear two things. One is that we have done over US$3m worth of business in minimum guaranteed payments from the film's distributors – triple the estimated amount – to which we would certainly have added another US$2m from the American rights had we not chosen to favour improved terms from Gramercy over a substantial advance from somebody else. The other is that we have won the Prix du Publique. Initially nobody is quite sure what this is, but we are delighted to win any prize, particularly one we did not realise existed, so we find out. About 20,000 local people who attend special pay-screenings of those movies shown in all official sections of the festival other than the competition vote for their favourite at the end. It is *Priscilla*.

Once initiated, momentum is completely self-propelling. The more capricious the business – and films and records are more so than most – the greater its tendency to oscillate wildly between catatonic inertia and deranged hyperactivity.

At the PolyGram managing directors' conference in Vancouver, from where we receive congratulatory faxes from both Michael Kuhn and Stewart Till, the soundtrack album that nobody wanted appears to have become the coveted trophy in an internecine bidding war. In this inflated boys' club of a setting, Polydor Australia has begun to show a strong proprietorial stance, prompted by the competitive interest of Island and Chris Blackwell and Mother Records and Paul McGuinness, whose own enthusiasm for the music was quickly broadcast after he saw the film in San Francisco. The clearances that appeared impossible to secure stray mysteriously into the realms of accomplishment.

Memos begin to fly around like heat-seeking missiles. Mother Records will originate and release the album on their label, distributed by Island in the US and Polydor elsewhere, including Australia. Stephan and I favour choosing a couple of tracks and having them radically remixed as singles by a London-based dance producer. Polydor consider this unnecessarily expensive, favouring instead a kind of retro party album without new mixes. They want Gloria Gaynor's 'I Will Survive' as the first single; we favour Alicia Bridges' 'I Love the Nightlife', particularly as a remixed reissue of Gaynor's record has already been in the British top five a year earlier.

Finally, it is concluded with Mother: there will be remixes, which can also be added to the soundtrack album. We are very confused about precisely who is doing what, and unsympathetic towards the scheduling and manufacturing pressures engendered by the need to meet the film's US release date ten weeks away. Everyone has had six months to prepare for this. The problem has been disregarded because it was believed that the album would never materialise without a senior executive in the corporation willing to be the flag bearer, which none of them were interested in being. In other words, until this point, there was a consensus of neglect.

Despite discussion of a major British release on October 14, no premiere is planned.

There is no question that vanity plays a significant part in the proclivity which most producers and directors have for the high-profile opening night. In our case – apart from having witnessed the remarkable boost it gave to the first weekend's box office of *Four Weddings and a Funeral* in the UK just before Cannes – we are also convinced that *Priscilla* is the kind of movie which, on the evidence of its two festival screenings to date, generates tremendous media interest and word-of-mouth from crowded special events.

Notwithstanding the success of the *Four Weddings* night, PolyGram claim that such openings are finally a waste of money. We feel that they are just trying to rationalise their innate fear of the potential for embarrassing misbehaviour which even the most sweet-natured drag queens carry around them like a flickering aura. Sensing the need to throw us a bone as we begin to leave incisions in their ankles, they propose having an opening at the MGM Trocadero. 'But doesn't that have a moving staircase leading to a small lobby?' I ask. Nobody appears certain but it is agreed that probably it has. 'You can't have celebrities photographed going up an escalator smiling as if they had all bumped into each other in a department store,' I exclaim in disbelief. 'And what about all the frocks getting caught in the teeth?' adds Stephan. 'We don't want our guests eaten before the film has even started.'

The Interlude

While PolyGram consider further, I return to my lodgings. Terence Stamp has lent me his apartment in Albany, a venerable old building set back from the road next to the Royal Academy on Piccadilly, whose discreet positioning and profound quiet bely the fact that it occupies an entire block of completely central London. Terence has lived in the place for nearly thirty years, most of them in this particular flat, which looks up at the rooftop on Savile Row where the Beatles last performed live in 1969. It is not really an apartment, or a flat, or even a duplex, although it meets the requirement by occupying two floors: it is more like 'rooms' or 'chambers', redolent of academic or legal life when these professions had gravity. He has decorated it with his customary taste and precision, a combination of Eastern asceticism (large, minimally decorated Japanese bedroom and tubroom) and Western comfort (Aga cooker, wooden kitchen, capacious sofa).

In a climate of such harmony, only the collisions really register: a collection of highly masculine, rigorously maintained shoes and boots, all in trees or bags, with at their centre the pair of custom-made Anello and Davide high heels in which Terence practised his walk before coming to Australia; shoes so perfectly timeless they might have been worn by his idol Gene Tierney, whose autographed photo still sits propped up against a wall in his dressing room.

One of the residents of Albany is the former cabinet minister Alan Clark, whose published diaries, of which I am unaware at this time, reveal that some ten years earlier he had affairs with the wife of a judge and her two daughters. Amidst allegations of blackmail and indecent

155

exposure, the judge, the wife and one of the daughters have arrived in London from South Africa to 'horsewhip' Mr Clark and sell their story to a newspaper. It appears that the judge's wife continued their affair even after she had discovered that Mr Clark had been having sex with both her daughters.

I arrive outside the building late one night to find a car full of reporters and photographers waiting at the entrance to the yard. A blonde woman in a raincoat jumps out and comes running across to me. 'Do you know Alan Clark?' she asks breathlessly. I hear Al. It is an irresistible moment. 'Of course I do,' I reply playfully, 'I *am* him.' For a fraction of a second, she looks simultaneously exhilarated and deflated, as if unable to believe that a stake-out at Albany could ever be so easy. I fantasise that she is a PolyGram commando whose mission is to seduce me out of the idea of having a *Priscilla* premiere.

'I have a feeling it's not me you're looking for,' I say when the moment is over. 'No,' she replies despondently, walking back towards her colleagues, ready to shoot herself. 'You're the wrong Al Clark. The right one is probably still in Jersey.'

An hour after the plane touches down in Los Angeles, I am driving to another press screening of the film. It is one of those dreamy, balmy LA evenings in early summer, before the cumulative sting of the sun and smog have become disagreeable. I have not wearied of watching the movie with different audiences, always enjoying the immediacy of the response to this kind of picture. With a comedy, there is no need to wait in the lobby for reactions afterwards: people tell you what they feel as they watch.

The Interlude

Balloting by audience members has been completed at the San Francisco Film Festival and we have won the Starbucks Award for the most popular film. Newly invited to the Seattle Festival, and hoping to witness the moment that may lead to a hat-trick of festival audience awards, I fly there the next day. The movie receives a vocally appreciative reaction, with the applause and cheers extending over the three minutes of end titles and beyond. When it is announced at the end of the festival that we have won the Golden Space Needle award for the best picture and Terence the best actor prize, I am finally confident that the response so far has not been the outcome of some collusion.

While I want the movie to make money, it is the fact that it gives *pleasure* which excites me, a pleasure-giving that in any case will lead to money at the box office. PolyGram are already going to do very well out of the film as sales agents and distributors, but my concern is the income which goes into the recoupment pot, to be shared first between the investors, then among all the profit participants. We need to monitor expenses carefully in order to accelerate the moment when those profit participants begin to defy film folklore by seeing a return.

Stephan is renewing his American visa. There is a section on 'inadmissible classes'. These include 'aliens who are mentally retarded, insane, or have suffered one or more attacks of insanity; aliens afflicted with psychopathic personality, sexual deviation, mental defect, narcotic drug addiction, chronic alcoholism or any contagious disease; aliens who are paupers, professional beggars or vagrants; aliens who are polygamists or advocate polygamy', and so on. It sounds like a chronicle of the people we have so far met in the United States.

Gramercy test two trailers to judge their effectiveness, or in survey-speak, their 'interest-generating potential'. Both tests are conducted by 'a personal intercept interviewing technique' among two hundred 'straight' moviegoers and one hundred 'gay, lesbian or bisexual' moviegoers, groups equally male and female of 18 to 49-year-olds, in 'four geographically dispersed urban markets' – Atlanta, New York, Philadelphia and San Francisco.

The first is a teaser trailer, intended for immediate release. The setting up of the joke revolves around the idea of extra-terrestrial invaders, the narrator's delivery recalling the golden age of American communist propaganda. 'If alien beings arrived in your town, how would they act ... what would they say ... and, most importantly, what would they wear?' People still capable of speech after the personal intercept interviewing technique has taken effect, are asked about awareness of and curiosity in the movie by the title and stars alone, then shown the teaser and asked about their interest as a consequence of it.

The title and stars appear not to have much interest-generating potential at all. Straights register 14 per cent, gays 27 (against a norm of 45). After seeing the trailer, however, while the straights only go up to 36 per cent, gays increase to 77 (norm 65). Two weeks later, a second, longer trailer – less of a tease, with added story elements – is more effective among straights, who increase to 45 per cent, but less among gays, who decline to a still resilient 72.

For the poster, Gramercy finally favour the concept of

silhouetting the rear view of the three drag queens against a sunset. Anticipating the effect that theatre-lobby poster-stall backlighting will have on it, I feel sure it will work but the colours need to be richer and more saturated than the proof suggests.

In addition to the post-production script we have already supplied as part of the delivery schedule, we are reminded by PolyGram that they also require a 'spotting' script, whose presence on the list of items I was sufficiently myopic to overlook. Where the final dialogue outlined in the post-production script is essential for dubbing purposes, a spotting script is a condensed version which conveys the essence of each section of dialogue. This enables subtitlers to disregard the nuances of what is being said in favour of the facile contraction.

We have also been asked for a glossary in which all the colloquialisms and abuse (in the case of our film, pretty much the same thing) are listed with their corresponding meaning. Among the seven pages of these we supply are numerous highlights, beginning with the first words of the film. A heckler in the audience has thrown a beer can at Mitzi (Hugo Weaving), knocking her over, so Felicia takes the microphone: 'That was fucking charming, you gutless pack of dickheads,' she says. Our translator's notes read: 'That's not very nice, you cowardly group of idiots.' When a few minutes into the film 'Fuck off you silly queer' becomes 'Go away you silly homosexual', we realise this is a document which will eventually be viewed as a seminal contribution to world understanding, or at least as a challenge to the skills of subtitlers everywhere:

Film Term	Meaning
pink bits	vagina
going bush	going to the country
ring pirate, doughnut puncher	homosexual
love handles	fatty hips
wing wang	penis
cracking a fat	getting an erection
fat slags	overweight women
abysmal batting average	no sex
bats for both teams	bisexual
tackarama	bad taste
ping pongs	testicles
dirty old fuck	deviant old man
nong	silly person
shut your twat	be quiet
come the raw prawn	try to mislead
the chop	operation to remove male genitals
cocksucker	person who engages in fellatio
hide the sausage	sexual intercourse

When the film goes to the ratings boards it receives an R in the US ('for sex-related situations and language') and an M, – recommended for people over 15 – in Australia ('medium-level coarse language and sexual references'). We are relieved that neither censor requests a glossary.

Two soundtrack album clearances are still proving difficult. The likelihood is that both R. B. Greaves' 'Take a Letter Maria' and Lena Horne's 'A Fine Romance' will be omitted from the record for cost reasons. As the payment of the film's synch licences is now being covered entirely by the FFC, and neither Polydor nor Mother are paying any advance to the movie, the penny-pinching is incomprehensible at this stage. What appears to be happening is that this soundtrack, an orphan until a few weeks earlier, and on which we lost further time while everybody worked out who was releasing it, now has the unmistakable whiff of money to the few song licensors who are outside the PolyGram group.

This – together with realising that we still do not have confirmation of who is doing the remixes, and that the sniffy initial reaction to Stephan's video concept has not been followed by any decisive feedback – makes us wonder if it really is worth the effort any more. When 'Maria' and 'Romance' are finally cleared – giving us the fourteen core-tracks plus remixes – we decide that it is.

The video of Alicia Bridges' 'I Love the Nightlife' is still not resolved. The consensus among the various record companies is that any attempt at storytelling other than through the film images is likely to confuse the viewer, and that if the video is to engender interest in the movie it should simply condense the film's narrative. 'Because the beats are so strong/clear in the song,' reads one memo, 'simply editing brilliant film images (of which there are many) in a compelling way to the sound bed may be a logical approach.' However, because the standards departments of MTV and similar channels insist that no more than 40 per cent of a video can be footage from a motion picture – at which point in their terms it becomes a movie advertisement rather than a record promotion –

this does not take into account who, if anyone, is going to perform the song to camera.

The Rapino Brothers remix arrives: a big disappointment. With my negligible knowledge of contemporary club sounds, it sounds all right to me, if a little anachronistic, ironically recalling the early days of Stock/Aitken/Waterman. Stephan dislikes it intensely and feels it epitomises what he and Mother in London had agreed should *not* be done. Neither of us believes it is a hit single. Stephan goes so far as to promise that he will eat his shoe if it reaches the top ten.

One of the difficulties in aiming for an of-the-moment remix of an old disco hit is that people can rarely agree on what it should sound like. The Charlene and R. B. Greaves songs, both eccentric in a timeless way, have an honest nostalgia about them which would get radio if not club play. In our bid to be contemporary, we may be missing the mark by a mile, and I do not enjoy the prospect of a flop single preceding what is showing signs of being a successful film. A second remix, done in New York by Phillip Damien, is better but still not right.

Someone finally disinters the original Alicia Bridges video, made in 1978, in which she looks like, as one viewer puts it, Billy Idol's mum. Rendered out of contention by its crude presentation, it will be impossible to use in any case because her movements do not match the tempo of the new mix. However, Stephan has an idea of how to incorporate it in his revised concept for the video which, stripped of its extravagant effects and armies of extras, is still wonderfully imaginative.

A matt full moon hangs over an affluent Sydney suburb, and superimposed on to it is Alicia Bridges singing to camera from a distance, which bypasses the tempo problem. We return to her occasionally but mostly we follow the gradual metamorphosis of airline pilot and family man Hugo Weaving into a drag queen dancing in the street with miniature planes in her epaulettes and propellers on her nipples. In the course of the transformation, drag images from *Priscilla* appear in the mirror, reflected in perfume bottles, even emerging from a lipstick as his alter ego takes over and he runs out of the house to lead an army of drag queens – who have emerged from neighbouring homes – through the moon-kissed streets.

We call it Drag Wolf. Polydor refer to it as Jekyll and Hyde and Hugo. The whole thing is shot in a day on a housing estate on the North Shore resembling a giant *Stepford Wives* set, with the crowd of drag queens and friends in the finale reinforced with curious locals. Towards the end of the day, Hugo falls down a flight of stairs in six-inch stilettos and tears a ligament in his ankle. For several nights, he goes on stage at the Sydney Opera House in Tom Stoppard's *Arcadia* with a limp, and extra emphasis is placed on a line in the play about his character being prone to driving into ditches.

A few days later, Stephan goes to America for a week-long publicity tour before the east coast premiere at the Hamptons. For a moment, it appears that a contractual oversight on their part is prompting Polygram to reconsider their release plan.

The moment passes. The buttons are pressed. We are on our way.

The American Premieres

Fetid, cranky, rumbustious, as infatuated with its 'energy' as the outsiders who perpetually rhapsodise about it, New York is a city running – to borrow the writer Mick Brown's indelible phrase about somewhere else – on the emergency tank of its own mythology.

Although only the defiantly hardcore East-Coasters of the movie business live there, the place increasingly resembles a giant film set in which 'Action!' has been called seconds before one's arrival and 'Cut!' moments after departure. The featured players and extras are seamlessly absorbed in the process and have chosen their roles with the unerring exactness of a casting director. There are occasional lapses in the wardrobe department: a couple of middle-aged businessmen jog down Sixth Avenue early one morning wearing white shorts over brightly coloured spandex tights, as if they have borrowed accessories from their wives' closets to help them come out of their own. As for the set design, the steam which rises with such evocative predictability out of the drains and subway grids has now been so sanctified by the New York films of the British commercials directors Adrian Lyne (*Flashdance, 9½ Weeks, Fatal Attraction, Jacob's Ladder*), Alan Parker (*Fame*) and Ridley Scott (*Someone To Watch Over Me*) that all too easily one can imagine thousands of stand-by props people with smoke machines running along a network of underground tunnels to keep the vapour topped up to appropriately pictorial levels.

Even the old panhandlers look like they might be the grandfathers of the character Eddie Murphy plays at the beginning of *Trading Places*, although racial jokes tend to get a frosty reception in this – when one considers its anarchic self-image – paradoxically conformist of cities, the style-sheet of whose principal newspaper the *New York Times* is a testament to a fear of causing offence, a treasury of linguistic cleansing and politically correct euphemisms. (A couple of years ago, it declared that the Massachusetts state budget had, for the first time in several years, gone into the African-American. It sportingly made a correction the following day: what the Massachusetts state budget had really done was go into the black.)

The East Coast premiere of *Priscilla* is being held not on a weekday in Manhattan – where, the theory goes, it would have played primarily to the media crowd, most of whom have already seen the film – but on a Friday night in the Hamptons, where it will be attended by the kind of celebrities who holiday there in the summer, and by those wealthy, taste-making New Yorkers who have left the city sufficiently early to struggle through the afternoon traffic of Long Island and arrive – a quick shower and change of clothes later – in time for the screening.

Gramercy's premise – reinforced by the publicist Peggy Siegal, who is organising the event – is that, as most of the people they would want to have at the New York show are in the Hamptons, we should bring the show to them. So we do.

It is to take place in Sag Harbor, a quaintly affluent, low-key tourist town favoured by artists and writers on the south fork of coastal Long Island. This was Indian territory when the whites began to settle three centuries ago. Then it became a seaport with a burgeoning whaling industry, abandoned when the whalers heard about the California goldfields. Now the people with their own California goldfields, like Steven Spielberg, go there to relax.

The guest list leans more towards East Coast aristocracy than movie celebrities – various Aga Khans, the designers Calvin Klein, Donna Karan and Marc Jacobs, show business tycoon David Geffen – and how this upscale bunch will respond to a downscale joke about an Abba turd is a moment one can barely wait to witness.

When the first Gramercy person arrived in town earlier in the week to test the print in the Sag Harbor Cinema, what he heard was so primitive that a Dolby engineer was airlifted in from New York to upgrade the sound system. And as Sag Harbor does not appear to have any of its own drag queens, we fly them in as well.

Greeting arrivals outside the theatre on the quiet main street in the diminishing evening light, they make a sensational trio, stopping the traffic intermittently, the jaws of pedestrians dropping as they approach. A few disappointed customers, anticipating the billed session of Kieslowski's *Three Colours White*, linger to watch the feathered and sequined creatures who have invaded the sidewalks of their town.

Stephan and Terence – criss-crossing on different legs of a US publicity tour – have flown, from Atlanta and Chicago respectively, into the small airport nearby one hour before the screening is scheduled to start, as have Russell Schwartz from Los Angeles and, from New York, Michael Kuhn and Alain Levy, the head of all PolyGram's entertainment interests, who is seeing the film for the first time.

Having witnessed in San Francisco and Seattle the kind of unbridled commotion that a fully engaged American audience can engender, I find the response to the movie disappointingly tentative. Walking down the street to the after-show party at a nightclub called the Amazon Deck, we stop in a bar for a drink, not so much to restore ourselves as to make a collective guess at wondering what we are all doing here.

When we arrive at the party Stephan is asked the same question by a reporter. 'I have absolutely no fucking idea whatsoever,' he replies. It is a brilliantly condensed summary of the bewilderment shared by several of us. My own bewilderment is exacerbated by the dislocating effects of twenty-one hours of air travel the day before, followed by a four-hour car drive that morning, the passenger of Stephan's agent Bobbi Thompson, as engaging a companion as she is a terrifyingly distracted driver. Since we know none of the four hundred guests at the party, we concentrate on keeping each other amused.

Stephan tells me that during a dinner in San Francisco he asked the former girlfriend of a now openly gay colleague what the first signs she noticed were. She came back without a beat: 'He kept turning me over.' While in Atlanta he discovered that Alicia Bridges, of whom little has been heard since 'I Love the Nightlife', lived there, so he decided to track her down. The trail led to an over-forties leather bar, full of men in peaked leather caps and bare-bottomed pants, where Alicia Bridges works as a disc-jockey one night a week, playing old disco records to old fistfuckers.

Despite the unsettling, thankfully temporary, loss of a prized purple sock while in Chicago, and a weariness about the demands of his schedule ('I am a prince, not a slave,' he tells Gramercy), Terence is in good spirits, and very much in his element here. He has been living in nearby Amagansett for some weeks in a windmill next to an organic farm, which must seem like being in heaven to him, and the party – hosted by *Hamptons Magazine* and Hugo Boss – is emphatically 'in honour of Terence Stamp'.

The pink invitation card has a feather and sequins in it, but at the party all one can see is the glitter which was sprinkled on everyone as they arrived at the theatre. Kuhn, covered in glitter, talking to the *New York Times*; Schwartz, covered in glitter, scanning the deck lasciviously; me, covered in glitter, delirious with jetlag, longing for bed, and wondering about the $26,000 worth of television advertising we could have bought instead. We are all getting drunk, and dealing with it in our different ways.

It seems that nobody in the place can stop talking, except for Alain Levy, who wanders around watching other people talk. In the encroaching penumbra, I begin to recognise a few faces. Griffin Dunne still has that slightly haunted look which suggests he no more wants to be stranded at the Amazon Deck than he did at the Club Berlin in the indelible punk nightclub sequence from *After Hours*. Marisa Tomei, a 1993 Oscar winner for *My Cousin Vinny*, is having her picture taken with Terence, who does not appear to know who she is. Stephan, in conversation with Bret Easton Ellis, tries his pitch of turning *American Psycho* into a musical on the author himself, who simulates polite but detached interest in a manner which the very famous, confident they will be interrupted within moments, have made their own. Tim Chappel, having completed the dressing of the *Priscilla* windows at the department store Barney's, has finally arrived on a late train from New York.

A menswear manufacturer from Philadelphia, whose yacht is moored in Sag Harbor, has called Gramercy and offered to pay several thousand dollars to 'buy into' the premiere party. When his offer is declined, he hires a PR woman who has been invited to scan the guests and find suitable companions for his yacht, which is moored adjacent to the venue.

It is virtually inconceivable for an Australian to pass up an invitation to a yacht party and, sure enough, they all go.

In a week when the US senate votes to cut off federal money to schools which teach acceptance of homosexuality as a way of life, the newspapers and magazines are full of drag queens, and not just ours. *To Wong Foo*, which has recently started shooting, is already riding on the coat-tails of our publicity, with pictures of Patrick Swayze in a beehive and a burgundy ballgown: much more the kind of 'lady' Terence had in mind before Lizzy and Tim showed him their costumes.

While walking along the street in New York, I notice that our old friend Vanessa Williams – who nearly prevented us from using her song 'Save the Best For Last' over the end titles after we had shot them to picture with a lip-synching Tim Chappel in drag – is appearing in a Broadway production of *Kiss of the Spiderwoman* playing, as one might expect, the movie goddess in the fantasies of a gay window dresser in a Latin American prison. A review in *Time* magazine says she makes a very wholesome siren: 'Any sensible fly would want to scuttle to the centre of her web and cuddle up.'

Scuttling to the centre of Lisa Marie Presley's web has been Michael Jackson, the confirmation of whose wedding, rumoured to have taken place some weeks back, has just been announced by Donald Trump to the reporters and tourists on the pavement outside his eponymous Tower, on the top floor of which the lovebirds – proclaiming their need for privacy – are allegedly holed up. While police in Los Angeles continue to investigate allegations by a thirteen-year-old boy that Jackson sexually molested him – an investigation later dropped – the local press are fascinated by the marriage 'conceived,' as one put it, 'in supermarket tabloid heaven,' and ask all the important questions. Are they both too strange to marry anybody else? Is she recruiting him for the celebrity-loving Church of Scientology? Most importantly, was Elvis at the wedding? A psychic claims gravely that 'Elvis doesn't want Jackson's gloved hand inside Graceland'.

Stephan, Grant and Tim arrive back in town full of funny stories about the party on the yacht, and about another one held on the runway of the local airport. We take a taxi downtown to look at the *Priscilla* clothes which, with a Chanel suit at the centre of each window, occupy the entire Seventh Avenue side of Barney's. Stephan and Tim go on to a club where a complete stranger begins a conversation by asking them if they would like to see his cock ring; then, without waiting for an answer, he unzips himself and shows it to them. Later, a drummer plays on a full kit in the middle of a crowded dance floor as a cat – some disco kitty, probably on drugs – roams around the legs of the dancers.

They have entered a realm of madness for which most people have lost the talent or appetite. 'Eroticism,' Roman Polanski once wrote, 'is when you use a feather and pornography is when you use the whole chicken.' In New York it seems, they always use the whole chicken.

I forgo a big promotional screening and a party afterwards featuring the by now inevitable drag show – which sounds like another lively night out – in favour of going to Los Angeles ahead of schedule. That is where mission control for the American launch is located, so that, I reason, is where I should be.

Cable advertising has already begun on most of the major channels and the 'Be a Frock Star' lip-synch/dress-up promotion (tag line: 'you don't need a great voice, just a great outfit') is being set up by Gramercy's local agencies in the top twenty-five markets around the country, with banners, flyers, table tents, napkins and coasters especially designed for the event. One of the prizes, called 'Queen For a Day', involves a trip to a beauty shop, manicurist or hairdresser.

Gramercy has studied the case histories of two pictures with similar 'genre' appeal – *Strictly Ballroom* and *The Crying Game* – and has prepared a full report, revealing for example that over 65 per cent of *Strictly Ballroom*'s US income came from four markets (New York, Los Angeles, San Francisco and Washington), and concluding that the film 'played extremely urban'. *The Crying Game*, meanwhile, expanded from an initial two-city platform release to sixty-six screens in its fifth week, which started on the Christmas weekend. Not long after came its Oscar nominations, and a month prior to the awards themselves the film finally went wide.

While we work at establishing a level of awareness of the film in the US, the newspaper articles I am faxed from Australia suggest there can be hardly anyone there who reads or watches television who is not conscious of the movie. It already feels that it may be one of those rare pictures which enters the national bloodstream and becomes part of the country's collective psyche.

This is soon reinforced by three things. The first is that *Priscilla* has been nominated for nine Australian Film Institute awards. The second is that we have a serious video piracy problem in Sydney and Melbourne. Cassettes are being screened at gatherings of various sizes, some of them charging admission. As well as being copyright theft, it is particularly aggravating to me, after going to such lengths during post-production to keep the film away from anyone other than essential crew members, that it can now be viewed on a television screen by anyone with connections on the party circuit. We employ a private detective to locate the source of the tapes. The third is that Bus Priscilla, which was parked in a Sydney street, has been stolen.

In Los Angeles, Gramercy are having a few bus problems of their own. They have rented a Metropolitan Transport Authority bus – which follows the same Santa Monica-Downtown route that the vehicle in *Speed* does – wrapped it in *Priscilla* advertising equally arresting to passengers and passers-by, and have found themselves immobilised by a transport strike, which fortunately looks like being resolved.

The bus will be taken off the road for a couple of hours on the night of our premiere, which I am reminded takes place on the twenty-fifth anniversary of the gruesome slaughter in Benedict Canyon of Sharon Tate and four visitors to her house by members of the Charles Manson gang. (One of the victims was the hairdresser Jay Sebring who, according to the *Los Angeles Times*, had among his clients David Geffen, whose Geffen Records recently released a Guns 'N' Roses album including a song written by Manson.) Manson is now viewed in some circles as a criminal anti-hero. Certainly nobody has had more of an effect in changing the social climate of a city, sending the famous scurrying behind locked doors, security patrols and bedside guns, an end for some time to celebrities smoking joints under the fairylights with long-haired strangers.

(The quarter-century memorial of the Manson killings takes O. J. Simpson off the front pages of newspapers for the only occasion that week, as America's fascination with its fallen hero continues. Another story concerns a chocolate maker in the San Fernando Valley who was approached by a mysterious friend of Michael Jackson's family, asked to make one thousand chocolate bars about the size of a business card, with raised letters spelling out 'Lisa Marie and Michael' next to a heart and a musical note, and then have them delivered to two Jackson family addresses, Graceland and the Trump Tower. The chocolate maker has already sold the exclusive days earlier to the television program *Hard Copy*. 'It's a fun story,' he says. 'It's not like I'm showing a picture of them on their honeymoon.')

It is also the twenty-fifth anniversary of Woodstock,

occasionally referred to in the press as Woodstock 90210, bespeaking its yuppified conversion from a piece of muddy spontaneous combustion to a highly regulated pay-per-view television event on which PolyGram Diversified Ventures (a cousin of our investor PolyGram Filmed Entertainment) is gambling thirty million dollars.

I have wanted to have a premiere at the Cinerama Dome in Los Angeles since I first started producing movies, which was four years after seeing *Apocalypse Now* there in 1979. With its eccentric, custom-built, 'theme building' shape, its enormous curved screen and extraordinary acoustics, it is a cinema which always increases the size of a big-looking picture and diminishes that of a small-looking one. Accordingly I saw *The Untouchables* there in 1987, but skipped *Honeymoon in Vegas* in 1992, preferring to wait until it arrived in its natural habitat, the multiplex.

It is a real premiere in a great movie theatre, not one of those Hollywood 'previews' where everyone goes in clutching their Evian bottles like liquid comfort blankets. Several members of the crew have flown in from Australia, and we gather in the car park behind the cinema in the softening twilight to see numerous drag queens, Terence, Guy and Stephan on to the bus which will deliver them to the crowd gathered around the front. It is one of those moments that, for all kinds of reasons, will never be duplicated.

As the bus needs to be sufficiently full for its arrival outside the theatre not to be anti-climactic, there are over twenty drag queens packed into it. While his life for the past few weeks has consisted of little more than travelling, talking and having his picture taken with the different drag queens who materialise in each town, Terence is holding up well. During the screening I have to pinch myself: our little movie is truly filling the huge Dome screen.

At the party afterwards, an early copy of Janet Maslin's rave in the following morning's *New York Times* ('Flamboyantly colourful, sweetly old fashioned') is already circulating, joined later by Kenneth Turan's less committed but largely positive one ('comic pizazz, bawdy dazzle') in the *Los Angeles Times*. Both praise Terence's performance, and the following day most of the other critics will also single him out, usually alluding to a potential Oscar nomination as well as to the actresses he purportedly resembles on screen: to the existing gallery are added Dorothy Malone, Faye Dunaway and Vivien Leigh.

At the bar, Paul Rosenfeld treats me to his opinion of a town where the picture will eventually play if we go wider than the main cities. 'It's a shit-hole of a place,' he declares peremptorily. 'It's where they plug the enema tube into America.' In the lobby, I am introduced to some of the gay aristocracy of LA. We have a completely ritualised conversation: they refuse to believe that Guy Pearce is straight, and I assure them he is.

I ask my driver for the night to take home a couple of weary friends with babysitting problems and return to collect me. In the meantime, the party closes down with such haste that it leaves the sybaritic Australian contingent stranded in mid-revel. Undeterred and in convoy, they move on to somewhere else. While I wait for the car to show up on a now deserted Vine Street, I lose my appetite for the extended party. It does not arrive during the ten minutes of endurance I have left. I hail what may be the only passing taxi in all of Los Angeles and go home.

We open in Australia four weeks later on September 8, then start rolling out across Europe, with Spain, Italy and all Scandinavia starting on September 30, the UK on October 14, and so on until the end of the year. The only territories in which the distributor prefers to wait until 1995 are France and Japan, where the availability of the right screens for what they consider an arthouse picture with crossover potential is always a problem.

Everybody seems to love the film. Everybody, that is, apart from Nathan Sanders, the publisher and editor of the US Abba Club fanzine. Mysteriously, he is deeply offended by the film's portrayal of Abba, which we consider benevolent in the extreme. Less mysteriously, given his chronic absence of irony, he dislikes the Abba fan represented by Guy Pearce, and he has written to Gramercy to tell them this. As part of the nationwide boycott of the movie that he is organising, he claims, he will contact over one million fan club members via fax, computer bulletin announcements, mailing lists and newsletters, and he will instruct them not to see it.

There is one element in particular which disturbs him. 'I find it a real stretch,' he writes, 'that this character, who can't be any older than twenty-five or twenty-six, saw Abba in concert and stole this "turd" out of the toilet that Agnetha Faltskog sat on. Abba's only live performance in Australia was in 1977. Was this character four years old when this event took place? Please! Don't insult our intelligence!' (Actually, the character would have been ten. Not that it matters. We would never allow plausibility to interfere with a good joke.) His sign-off is a classic of this kind of correspondence: 'This won't be the last you will hear from Abba fans on this matter.'

He also calls Liz Smith, the *New York Newsday* columnist, who quotes him as saying that he found the picture 'disappointing and disgusting ... particularly the &%$!-in-the-toilet business.' Liz is unable to bring herself to tell us what &%$! is. 'We'd rather not explain this,' she writes demurely. 'Go see the film if you must know.' After all the acceptance it has received, it is reassuring to know that there is something in the movie which can still get up people's noses.

Just before I leave Los Angeles to return to Sydney, with the first week's American box-office figures still buoyant in my system, I hear that one of the Sag Harbor drag queens got so trashed at the Amazon Deck party that she went back to her hotel, fell asleep and pissed all over the mattress. We have been sent a bill for the replacement.

After millions of dollars, thousands of miles, hundreds of hurdles, dozens of screenings, it is as if the drag queens who failed to show up for the casting sessions have finally demanded an absurd metaphor to bring the whole thing to a conclusion: a sodden mattress, for which somebody else must pay.

Perfect. Just perfect.